Feminist Criminology
through a Biosocial Lens

Feminist Criminology through a Biosocial Lens

Anthony Walsh

PROFESSOR, DEPARTMENT OF CRIMINAL JUSTICE,
BOISE STATE UNIVERSITY

CAROLINA ACADEMIC PRESS
Durham, North Carolina

Library of Congress Cataloging-in-Publication Data

Walsh, Anthony, 1941-
  Feminist criminology through a biosocial lens / Anthony Walsh.
     p. cm.
  Includes bibliographical references and index.
  ISBN 978-1-59460-966-4 (alk. paper)
  1. Feminist criminology. 2. Criminal behavior--Genetic aspects. 3. Crime--
Sex differences. 4. Sociobiology. I. Title.

  HV6030.W34 2011
  364.3'74--dc22

                    2010050830

CAROLINA ACADEMIC PRESS
700 Kent Street
Durham, North Carolina 27701
Telephone (919) 489-7486
Fax (919) 493-5668
www.cap-press.com

Printed in the United States of America

Contents

Foreword

Criminological research has produced very few "facts" about crime that are generally agreed upon by the majority of researchers in the field. One of the main exceptions to this general rule is the link between gender and crime. In virtually every single study ever conducted, males are much more likely than females to engage in violence, aggression, and serious crimes. As the seriousness of the offense/behavior increases, the gender gap also tends to increase, such that the most violent criminal acts are almost exclusively a male phenomenon. These findings have been produced by analyzing samples collected from different countries, at different time periods, and that include different racial/ethnic groups. The gender-crime nexus, in short, is robust, consistent, and not due to a methodological or statistical artifact.

That there is a connection between gender and crime is not disputed by any serious scholar of crime; however, the underlying mechanisms that account for males being much more criminal than females has been at the center of some serious and contentious debates. Explanations of the gender gap in offending, for example, range from differences in the ways boys and girls are socialized by their parents to differences in how the media depicts and portrays males and females. Regardless of which theoretical camp one belongs to, the overarching theme cutting across virtually all criminological explanations is that the only factors that could potentially account for the male-female gap in offending are environmental factors. To say otherwise would be blasphemous and heretical and would quickly incite the PC police into action.

The main problem with the theories designed to explain the gender gap in offending is that they are relatively defunct of empirical support and have provided virtually no insight into the causal processes that lead from gender to criminal involvement. Take, for example, theories that argue that the gender gap in offending can be tied to differences in family dynamics. The merits of such explanations hinge on whether or not parents treat their sons and daughters differently; if they do not, then there is no way that family socialization patterns could explain the huge gender disparity in offending. Vast amounts of research have examined potential gender differences in parental socialization tactics and across hundreds of studies there is very little evidence that parents socialize their children differently based on their gender. Even with this evidence in hand, criminologists continue to champion environmental explanations as they are viewed as safe, progressive, and liberating. Any other explanations—especially ones that incorporate findings from the biological sciences and from evolutionary research—are outright rejected because of the fear that they could be used in evil and dangerous ways. The point is that ideology and political correctness have been placed above objective science when it comes to studying gender differences.

Enter Anthony Walsh's book, *Feminist Criminology through a Biosocial Lens*. Unlike other books that treat the gender-crime association with kid gloves, Walsh tackles the gender gap in offending head-on using an empirically informed biosocial perspective that highlights the roles of environmental, genetic, neurobiological and evolutionary factors in the creation of male-female differences in criminal behavior. Walsh takes the reader on a journey through the emerging field of biosocial criminology and then uses findings from this line of research to provide a logically argued and empirically sound explanation of gender and crime that is free of the political and ideological pressures that most criminologists writing in this area succumb to. Most importantly, however, is that it provides testable hypotheses and falsifiable ideas which will spark the scientifically oriented criminologist to examine empirically, not rhetorically. The true impact that this book will have on the study of gender differences in crime will ultimately hinge on the results of empirical studies. When all is said and done, *Feminist Criminology through a Biosocial Lens* will likely stand out as perhaps the single-most accurate and important treatise on the gender-crime association published to date.

Kevin M. Beaver
Florida State University

Preface

According to Bernard, Snipes, and Gerould (2010:299) the issue of why always and everywhere males commit more criminal acts than females is the "single most important fact that criminology theories must be able to explain." While the centrality of the gender ratio issue to criminology is not in question, one could question the utility of continuing trying to answer it with the same conceptual and theoretical tools that have not proven useful in this regard. Gottfredson and Hirschi (1990:149) have even concluded that an explanation of gender differences in criminal behavior from the dominant sociological perspective is "beyond the scope of any available set of empirical data." This book offers an alternative to the strict environmentalism of the sociological perspective. It explores feminist criminology in general and attempts to explain its two central concerns—the generalizability and gender ratio problems—from a biosocial perspective. The biosocial paradigm is growing in strength every year, as an examination of both the number of published books and articles in professional journals in criminology and other social and behavioral science disciplines will attest.

Francis Cullen, one of criminology's most revered figures, calls the biosocial perspective "a broader and more powerful paradigm [than the sociological paradigm]" (2009:x). While there are many books on the market addressing female offending, most of them are too wedded to the single discipline of sociology; a kind of discipline reductionism is no longer acceptable. By way of contrast, this book ranges across sociology, anthropology, psychology, behavioral and molecular genetics, the neurosciences, and evolutionary biology. It is time to apply this exciting and robust paradigm—one that avers that *any* trait or behavior of *any* living thing is *always* the result of biological factors interacting with environmental factors—to the most vexing issues of feminist criminology.

Chapter 1 introduces the reader to the biosocial approach by focusing on Nobel Prize winner Nikolas Tinbergen's famous four questions. These questions are deemed necessary to ask if we are to understand the behavior of any organism because they urge us to look at current behavior from the most distal to the most proximate level of analysis. Feminism, what the movement is and what it is trying to accomplish is explored, followed by an introduction to the concept of gender. Gender is central to the concerns of this book and is only briefly touched on here. This is followed by a look at patriarchy from the points of view of both social constructionist feminists and evolutionary feminists.

Chapter 2 addresses feminist criminology's so-called generalizability problem, which asks if theories formulated, tested, and evaluated, and gleaned from male samples are applicable to females. I look at Eileen Leonard's examination of anomie, subcultural, differential association, labeling, and Marxist theories relevant to this issue (she concludes that none of them are fully applicable to female offending). Female-centered "mini-theories" such as *criminalizing girls' survival* and *victim precipitated homicide* designed to explain the crimes of girls and women as functions of their victimization by males are addressed. I then conclude that the generalizability problem is not a problem because female offenders are found in the same demographic locations and life situations as male offenders, and the same demographics and the same individual characteristics that predict male offending also predict female offending.

Chapter 3 examines the gender gap in criminal offending from a sociological point of view. Attitudinal and behavioral differences among classes of individuals (including gender) are almost invariably attributed exclusively to differences in socialization patterns by most sociologists. The first issue discussed in this chapter is thus gender socialization. I then address the possible role of the women's liberation movement in generating female offending by discussing the masculinization, emancipation, and economic marginalization hypotheses put forward by feminist criminologists. These hypotheses have come to be known collectively as the *convergence hypothesis*. The convergence hypothesis asserts that cultural changes leading to greater freedom for women will eventually lead them to commit crimes at rates close to male rates. I then look at evidence addressing this possibility.

Chapter 4 looks at power-control theory, a theory that explains gender differences in offending with reference to family dynamics, and structured action theory, which posits that excessive male offending is a function of how males "do gender." Both theories are based on socialization practices and say nothing about individual traits. There are explanations of gender differences based on differences in quantitative traits such as aggression and empathy, but once again these "explanations" turn exclusively to socialization to account for them. The final part of the chapter makes a plea to bring biology into the issue by examining what some prominent sociologists have said about doing so. I also identify a number of feminist biosocial scientists to show that feminism is far from incompatible with a biosocial perspective.

Chapter 5 discusses the concept of social constructionism and three philosophical concepts which its adherents abhor—determinism, essentialism, and reductionism. I begin by agreeing that in some sense everything is socially constructed because nature does not come to us ready labeled—humans must interpret it and stick labels on it through social agreement. I look at what constructionism has to offer us, and what we should avoid about it. I than examine the "triad of evils," showing how those who belong to the strong school of social constructionism seriously misunderstand these concepts, all of which are in many ways part of the foundation of modern science. I explain what these things are, what their value is, and how they are misunderstood.

Chapter 6 examines the social construction of gender, focusing on the strong social constructionist position that gender socialization patterns observed in a particular culture are arbitrary. It examines the powerful seductive appeal of social constructionism, concluding that its appeal lies in the extreme range of positions it allows its adherents to take relative to the much narrower range allowed by empirical science. I examine the gender-socialization-as-arbitrary position with reference to Margaret Mead's famous work on sex and temperament and its critics, as well as Melford Spiro's studies of the Israeli kibbutzim. I note that both Mead and Spiro came to reject their earlier cultural determinism for a more realistic biosocial position. This chapter is the transition chapter from the sociological to the biosocial.

Chapter 7 discusses the evolutionary origins of gender and establishes the foundation for claims that males and females have different rates of crime and other forms of antisocial behavior because they have evolved different natures. I begin by looking at human nature (and its denial on the part of social constructionists) and move on to how human nature is the sum of our evolutionary adaptations that have been captured by natural selection. Natural selection produces a sex-neutral human nature due to the common evolutionary concerns of both sexes; sexual selection produces a male nature and a female nature due to sex-specific evolutionary concerns. I then look at the selection pressures for biparental care (very rare among mammals) and how it prevented "runaway sexual selection" and moved male and female natures closer together in terms of their personalities and behavior.

Chapter 8 looks at evolutionary explanations for gender differences in criminality. The first of these explanations is Anne Campbell's "staying alive" hypothesis, which has to do with the male/female asymmetry in parental investment and how this led to sex differences in fear and status-striving. Shelly Taylor's tend-and-befriend hypothesis is then explored. This is a biobehavioral model of sex-differentiated responses to stress which have been forged due to the different reproductive roles of males and females. Finally, I look at three evolutionary theories of criminal behavior that focus on gender differences in offending. Each of these theories—cheater theory, conditional adaptation theory, and alternative adaptation theory—have as their organizing principle sex differences in reproductive strategies; that is, mating versus parenting effort.

Chapter 9 examines the neurohormonal basis of gender. The male brain is "sexed" in utero via the saturation of androgen receptors with androgens; the female brain remains in the default state of all mammalian brains—female. The SRY gene found on the Y sex chromosome initiates a series of processes that develops the XY embryo into a male. But this process can go wrong for a variety of reasons, leading to individuals whose gender identity is incongruent with their genital status. These individuals are known as intersex anomalies or pseudo-hermaphrodites, and I explore what they can tell us about the relative impact of prenatal hormonal surges versus socialization with regard to gender identity formation. These anomalies range from the complete insensitivity of androgen receptors, in which case chromosomal males develop as ultra-feminine females both physically and psychologically, to individuals with approximately twice the normal level of androgens.

Chapter 10 continues to explore sex differences in the brain. I first look at the neuroscience concepts of experience-expected and experience-dependent brain development to show that while the brain is "sexed" in utero, how it develops throughout life is an experience-dependent process. I then look at brain laterality and what it means for a variety of sex/gender differences in traits and behaviors. Arousal levels are then addressed in terms of sex/gender differences, followed by gender biases in the visual system. Apparently, many of the early sex-differentiated color and toy preferences that are often dismissed as gender stereotypes have their origins in different retinal cell densities of female-biased parvocellular cells and magnocellular cells in males. The brain differences examined in this chapter are linked to sex-differentiated roles in evolutionary history. Finally, I look at the different outcomes often experienced by males and females as the result of protracted stress which lead to externalizing and internalizing problems, respectively.

Chapter 11 looks at gender differences in major traits widely regarded as protective factors against antisocial behavior. The first trait is altruism, an active regard for the well-being of another, followed by empathy, a cognitive/emotional trait that motivates altruistic behavior. The evolutionary reasons why empathy is so important to women, such as the need to respond reflexively to infants' needs, are explored. I then look at the empirical evidence from endocrinology, neurobiology, and sundry other disciplines for the assertion that women are, on average, more empathetic and altruistic than males. I then look at guilt proneness and again find that females are higher than males on this prosocial trait. The final traits examined are from psychology's "big five" model—agreeableness and conscientiousness. Large worldwide studies have found that women exceed men on these traits in almost all cultures examined.

The final chapter reverses Chapter 11 by looking at gender differences in traits known to be strongly related to criminal behavior. These include impulsiveness, ADHD and ADHD/CD comorbidity, alcoholism, and psychopathy. Gender differences in all these antisocial traits are examined in terms of empirical data from many disciplines, all of which find that robust gender differences in them are ubiquitous across cultures. This chapter also contains an overall general conclusion section, with the primary conclusion being that we have every reason to *expect* large gender differences in criminal behavior and other forms of antisocial behavior. The gender ratio problem is really only a source of puzzlement to those who think of human beings as blank slates blown hither and thither like so many dead leaves by environmental winds. Indeed, it would be a major puzzle if we were to find a culture in which the female rate of criminal offending was approximately equal to the male rate.

Acknowledgments

I would first of all like to thank Carolina Academic Press, specifically Beth Hall, in acquisitions, for her faith in this project from the beginning. Thanks also for the commitment of Zoë Oakes. This tireless duo kept up a most useful three-way dialog between author, publisher, and excellent reviewers. My copy editor, Suzan Raney, spotted every errant comma, dangling participle, and missing reference and misspelled word in the manuscript, for which we are truly thankful. Production editor Kelly Miller made sure everything went quickly and smoothly thereafter. Thank you one and all.

Thanks to my colleague Dr. Lisa McClain, director of the gender's studies program at Boise State University for reading and critiquing parts of the manuscript. I am also most grateful for the reviewers who spent considerable time providing me with the benefit of their expertise. I also want to thank Hailey Johnson for her expert indexing of this and other books of mine. She is already a legend for writing the most intellectually courageous thesis ever attempted at Boise State University's Criminal Justice Department—the epigenetics of drug addiction, no less!

Most of all I would like to acknowledge the love and support of my most wonderful and drop-dead gorgeous wife, Grace Jean; aka "Grace the face." Grace's love and support has sustained me for so long that I cannot imagine life without her; she is a real treasure and the center of my universe.

Feminist Criminology
through a Biosocial Lens

Chapter 1

Feminist Criminology: Perspective and Concepts

The Biosocial Perspective and Tinbergen's Four Questions

Why are males so much more inclined to commit all sorts of antisocial, deviant, and criminal acts than females? Feminist criminologists and others have debated for decades about why the gender gap in criminal behavior has persisted across all historical periods and cultural contexts. They have been doing so almost exclusively within the sociological paradigm, which means that they have been limited to looking at socialization practices, social roles, and cultural values, norms, and practices. They have enjoyed very little success for all their efforts. As Gottfredson and Hirschi (1990:149) have concluded, an explanation of gender differences from this paradigm may be "beyond the scope of any available set of empirical data." This impotence is arguably because in this age of scientific ecumenicalism our "available" data sets in criminology, with some notable exceptions, remain parochial to the core.

The biosocial paradigm, on the other hand, is fundamentally ecumenical because it recognizes and affirms completely in theory and in practice that human beings are both biological and social animals. This is one of the reasons that prompted eminent philosopher of science Ian Hacking (2006:81) to write: "Biosocial is a new word, but its pedigree, although brief, is the best." The biosocial paradigm is being applied in all human disciplines, including criminology. One of criminology's leading luminaries, Francis T. Cullen, a longtime proud proponent of the sociological paradigm, has become "persuaded that sociological criminology has exhausted itself as a guide for the future study on the origins of crime. It is a paradigm for the previous century, not the current one" (2009:xvi). He describes the biosocial paradigm as "a broader and more powerful paradigm," and predicts that it will be the paradigm of the 21st century (2009:xvii). Given the admitted failure of the sociological paradigm to

3

make any sort of sense of the huge and perennial male/female gap in criminal behavior, it behooves feminist criminology to enter into the new age of biosocial criminology.

The biosocial approach is being so well received in so many disciplines because it is a powerful approach for examining all kinds of behaviors. It is a powerful approach because it examines behavior from all angles ranging from neurons to neighborhoods (Wright & Boisvert, 2009). This approach was advocated by Nobel Prize winning ethologist Nikolas Tinbergen long before the term *biosocial* was coined. Tinbergen (1963) maintained that to understand the behavior of any animal, including *Homo sapiens*, we have to ask four questions:

1. **Function:** What is the adaptive function of this behavior; i.e., how does this behavior contribute to reproductive success.
2. **Phylogeny:** What is the evolutionary history of the behavior? How did it come to have its current form?
3. **Development:** How do genes and environments interact in individuals to develop variation in this behavior?
4. **Causation:** What are the causal mechanisms that trigger this behavior?

To give a brief example of all levels let us consider a situation in which helping behavior (altruism) is elicited. The *Causation* question asks what the immediate mechanisms underlying altruistic behavior are. Altruism is motivated by an empathetic understanding of why someone needs help, and empathy is underlain by certain kinds of neurons, hormones, and neurotransmitters which we will discuss in Chapter 11. Performing the altruistic act facilitates the release of other chemicals that target the reward areas of the brain, and thus the helper is reinforced internally, as well as externally by the enhancement of his or her reputation in the eyes of others.

The *Development* question asks how this behavior became so strong in one individual's lifetime and so weak in another's. Although there are strong genetic influences on altruism and empathy via the chemical "machinery" that underlie them, the behaviors are developed (cultivated or neglected) via socialization, mimicry, and of course by the process of reinforcement conditioning outlined in the causation question.

The *Phylogeny* question asks how this behavior came about in the course of evolution. Parental care and mother-child bonding surely serve as the template for later social behavior, including helping behavior that aids in forging social bonds with others.

The *Function* question asks what the adaptive features of helping behavior are; what are the fitness consequences of helping. Helping others helps the self because it leads to reciprocal altruism. Mutual support aids all involved in avoiding predators, cooperative hunting and gathering, and many other features of social life, and because these things have obvious fitness consequences there will be strong selection pressures for them.

The function and phylogeny questions are ultimate level "why" questions and the development and causation questions are proximate "how" questions. We might even break down Tinbergen's levels even further as criminologist Matthew Robinson (2004) has done. Robinson examines criminal behavior moving from the lowest level (the molecular) and passing through the cellular, organ, individual, group, and community to the highest (society). All Tinbergen's questions and Robinson's levels of analysis are equally important and emphasize that there are no clear dividing lines in knowledge. An understanding of behavior cannot be reduced to the propositions of one discipline whose boundaries are arbitrarily drawn and closely guarded by university departments. Of course, no one carries out a research agenda animated by all Tinbergen's questions, but all levels have to be mutually consistent from top to bottom. No biologist, for example, would hypothesize a relationship between a hormone and a neurotransmitter that contradicts the known chemistry of those substances, just as no chemist would advance a hypothesis that contradicts the elegant laws of physics. Likewise, no hypothesis about a behavior or system of behavior at a higher level of analysis should contradict what is understood at a more fundamental level; i.e., the level enjoying the greater "hardness" (consensus, certainty) of its theories, methods, and data.

Feminism

Feminism is a social movement organized around the demand for social, political, and economic equality of the sexes/genders. Anne Campbell (2006:63) writes that no less than nine different strands of feminism have been identified that we can broadly divide into three major groups. She identifies "*social constructionists* (who reject scientific method as commonly understood) and liberals (who accept scientific method but seek to redress the past anthropocentrism of the topics studied and conclusions reached)." She further splits the liberals into *environmental liberals* who view gender differences as the result of gender socialization, and *evolutionary liberals*, who see gender differences built on the edifices of Darwinian natural and sexual selection. Campbell, a self-defined evolutionary liberal feminist, has made huge contributions to feminist biosocial criminology.

From the outset I must state that this work is aimed at feminists who retain their faith in science and follow the data wherever they lead, regardless of whether or not what they reveal is congenial to their political agenda. According to a survey of academic psychologists by Rhoda Unger (1996), most self-identified feminists reject traditional science, viewing it as an outdated patriarchal method of acquiring knowledge that is unsuitable to the feminist enterprise. This book is not for them. To my knowledge there have been no subsequent studies assessing the question of feminist attitudes toward science, but from personal observations I do not see explicit anti-science attitudes in feminist academics of my acquaintance. I do, however, note a rather strong hostility toward biological science when used to explore gender differences. This is no doubt because most feminists share the view with many other social scientists that biology connotes deterministic fixity. If this is their view of the role of biology in human behavior, then I can understand and sympathize with it, but it is a completely erroneous view. This is the kind of hostility I endeavor to counter in this book by showing that feminism has nothing to fear from biology and everything to gain by allying itself with a very robust, and indeed, friendly, collaborator. This is particularly true for feminist criminology with its primary focus on trying to understand the male-female crime gap.

Feminists employ a set of theories and strategies for social change in directions that improve the lot of women in ways consistent with these demands (Flavin, 2001). Feminism has a number of things in common with Marxism; the most pertinent is that both are social movements and worldviews in which criminology is only a small part. Also like Marxism, the general theoretical stance of feminism is highly critical of the social, political, and economic status quo. Feminism takes as a central theme the oppression and discrimination suffered by women in a society run for men by men who have passed laws and created customs, norms, and values designed to perpetuate their privileged position. Most females have accepted their position in life as normal, natural, and inevitable, and thus in common with Marx's proletariat, they suffer from a false consciousness undergirded by patriarchy (Irwin & Chesney-Lind, 2008). The core concepts and concerns of feminism (the need for wide social change, the nature of gender and patriarchy, oppression, false consciousness, and so forth) have been taken by feminist criminologists and applied to their work in the same way that the core elements of Marxism have been appropriated by Marxist criminologists. The most salient of these core concepts are gender and patriarchy. Both of these concepts are explored throughout the book, but will be briefly introduced and defined in this chapter.

Gender

One cornerstone of feminist criminology and feminism in general is the concept of gender. The use of the term "gender" was traditionally used to refer to the masculine and feminine grammatical categories of language, but sometime in the 1960s it came to be used to refer to categories of human males and females (Nicholson, 1994). Gender is often used as a synonym for sex (useful to avoid connotations of copulation), and when asked to check gender on forms and questionnaires the answer categories provided for us are "male" and "female." For social scientists, however the terms sex and gender refer to different but overlapping concepts. *Sex* refers to a person's biological status as a male or female and is used when making distinctions such as different chromosomal and gonadal status, different gamete and hormonal production, and different reproductive roles. *Gender* refers to social or cultural categories about how femininity and masculinity are molded and expressed in a particular culture, subculture, or situation in a particular historical time. The relationship between sex and gender is like that between genotype and phenotype, the latter being the result of the raw material provided by the former interacting with its physical, social, and cultural environment to produce the observable and measurable phenotype. Thus, while sex, with some rare exceptions, is a universal in its sameness, gender is a fluid and dynamic social construction built upon the superstructure of sex, although some of the more extreme social constructionist feminists may not accept that gender is based on anything material.

Gendered behavior will be examined with all four of Tinbergen's questions in mind. Male- and female-related behaviors that transcend cultures and historical periods had to have had some adaptive function in terms of the perennial concerns of all living things—survival and reproductive success. We also have to account evolutionarily for why these behaviors are gender-differentiated (gender-*related*, not gender-*specific*). In developmental terms we have to examine how socialization practices and cultural and subcultural expectations interact with predispositions to produce various levels of masculinity and femininity and modes of expressing gender identity. And finally, we have to look the genetic, neurobiological, and hormonal mechanisms that underlie gendered behavior. How a person "does gender" relies on all of the things, and thus we should not privilege one level over the other. The only criticism I offer throughout this book is not leveled at any one disciplinary level of analysis, only at those who want to gift that level exclusively and reduce all of their explanations to it.

Patriarchy

Patriarchy literally means "rule of the father," and is a term used to describe any social system that is male dominated at all levels from the family to the highest reaches of government and supported by the belief of overall male superiority. A patriarchal society is one in which "masculine" traits such as competitiveness, aggressiveness, autonomy, and individualism are lauded, and "feminine" traits such as intimacy, connection, cooperation, nurturance, while appreciated, are downplayed (Grana, 2002). Patriarchy occupies the same despised place among most feminist scholars that capitalism occupies among Marxists. The owners of the means of production (the *bourgeoisie*) are the oppressors in Marxist theory; the owners of the means of *re*production (all men) are the oppressors in feminist theory. This does not mean that women are powerless in patriarchy, only that the most powerful roles in most sectors of society are held predominantly by men and that men's privileged positions are institutionalized by law and custom.

Feminists believe that law is a mirror of patriarchal society and it has been used to devalue and disenfranchise women. Patriarchies, which means every society ever known, have used the law as a control mechanism to assure male dominance over women and girls, largely by codifying claims of female incompetence and by demonizing female sexuality. This has been taken to inhumane levels at times, such as the fashioning of chastity belts and the practice of female genital mutilation by either clitorectomy (removal of the clitoris) and/or infibulations (a ghastly "chastity belt" of thick fibrous scar tissue formed after the vagina is scraped and sewn together so that the vaginal opening is mostly closed until marriage). These practices occur in some Muslim countries even today.

These and other practices make it obvious that males have a deep concern about the possibility of cuckoldry, so natural selection would doubtless have selected genes that underlie traits that would incline them to monitor the behavior of females with whom they have invested resources. Darwinian feminist sociologist Rosemary Hopcroft (2009) proposes that the relatives of both males and females in a sexual relationship have interests in policing the sexual behavior of females since both sides have reproductive interests. The relatives of a male are interested in his paternal certainty, and the relatives of the female are interested in continued male investment in her offspring. These un-consciously motivated behaviors forged by eons of natural selection, Hopcroft maintains, are brought to the surface in the form of values, norms, and laws that control female sexuality in the service of male paternal certainty.

A number of views have been expressed about the origins of patriarchy and its universality. For most feminists, patriarchy as a system had its beginning in history as a man made institution, and as such can be changed by collective action. For those who subscribe to this "patriarchy as creation" idea, the origin was the development of agrarian cultures and with the sense of property ownership that they generate. This sense of property rights over land and animals evolved into a sense of property rights over wives and daughters. For instance, Gerda Lerner (1986) sees the basic sexual division of labor (women the producers of life, men the producers of goods) beginning about 5,000 to 10,000 years ago as the historical beginning of patriarchy. Language makes possible the ideologies and laws that have served to culturally elaborate, justify, and cement patriarchy.

For others, patriarchy is a natural phenomenon based on fundamental biological differences (size, strength, aggressiveness) between males and females and thus will never fundamentally change, although modes of patriarchal control can be muted. Darwinian feminists such as sociologist Joan Huber (2008) combine biological differences such as these with Lerner's sexual division of labor thesis. Huber theorizes that the origins of patriarchy are deeply connected with the evolutionary trajectory toward greater intelligence. Greater intelligence required bigger brains, and bigger brains required greater nutrition. This nutrition was provided to infants almost exclusively by breast milk until the 20th century when the water supply became safe enough to allow for bottle feeding. Adequate nutrition required that infants be breastfed every 15 minutes for a period of at least two years, and sometimes four, after which the mother probably became pregnant again in a continuous cycle of gestation and lactation. This biologically-imposed necessity meant that: "For nearly all of human history, gestation and prolonged lactation in the ancient mode [every 15 minutes] barred women from politics and warfare" (Huber, 2008:9). In other words, women were barred from public life first by virtue of her reproductive role, and later also by customs and laws that justified their exclusion. Modern reproductive technology in the form of birth control devices, breast pumps, and baby feeding formula are increasingly freeing women from their ancient, yet vitally important reproductive burden.

Note that both Hopcroft's (2009) and Huber's (2008) models rely on the bedrock of reproductive concerns that are different for males and females. This implies the inevitability and desirability of the patriarchal control of women because, after all, the term *natural* is often used synonymously with *good* or *de-*

sirable in everyday language. To conflate these terms (which neither Hopcropt nor Huber do, I hasten to say) is to commit what philosophers of science call the *naturalistic fallacy;* the fallacy of confusing *is* with *ought. Nature simply is,* what *ought* to be is a moral judgment. Needless to say, scientists must make the distinction between establishing facts and morally evaluating them. To claim patriarchy is a natural phenomenon is no more a moral statement than to claim that disease, death, floods, earthquakes, and other natural disasters which are unwelcome facts of life are natural phenomena. A number of morally repugnant traits that lead to morally repugnant practices have been selected for because of their fitness value, but this fact does not constitute a moral argument for or against any of them. Evolution is morally blind to its selections. It is a mindless algorithmic process that selects traits that enhance fitness regardless of how repugnant they may be. The impeccable logic of evolution helps to illuminate the ultimate reasons why these traits exist, and perhaps even suggest ways to control them. As I have maintained elsewhere (Walsh, 2009:64): "It is incumbent upon us to control immoral behaviors regardless of whether or not scientists show them to be products of natural selection, because just as *natural* does not mean *desirable*, it does not mean *inevitable*."

Feminist Criminology

Feminist criminology is situated squarely in the critical camp of criminology. Just as there are many varieties of critical criminology and of feminism in general there are many varieties of feminist criminology, and they are just as hard to capture with a single stroke of the pen. Because this is a book about the major issue of feminist criminology, not feminism per se, rather than split hairs I accept Campbell's trichotomized view of feminist positions. All approaches have at least one thing in common with "male" critical criminology; that is their opposition to mainstream patriarchal culture. The extent of the opposition varies according to the faction: Marxists want revolution, liberals will settle for reform. Feminist criminologists shift their emphasis from Marx's class and power to gender and power, although Marxist feminists add gender to class and view women as doubly oppressed by gender inequality generated by a sexist culture and by class inequality generated by a capitalist mode of production. Class-based conflict in the context of capitalism, however, largely gives way to gender-based conflict within the context of a patriarchal society, and the bourgeoisie and powerful interest groups so excoriated by male critical theorists become gendered, and defined as "rich white *men*" (Sokoloff & Price, 1995:14; emphasis original).

But what does all this have to do with crime? Since crime is overwhelmingly a male activity, why should criminologists bother with examining any effects that capitalism and patriarchy may have on female criminality? For those females who do criminally offend, why should their paths differ from those taken by male criminals? Are females' social experiences and ways of thinking so different that we need "special" theories of crime causation for them? These are questions often asked by feminist criminologists, and their answers are complex.

The primary complaint of feminist criminologists is that female crime has been virtually ignored by mainstream criminology, and despite the fact that women are responsible for only a small proportion of crime, feminists want to draw on women's "ways of knowing" to explain it (Daly & Chesney-Lind, 1988:490). Feminist criminologists thus want to put women on the criminological agenda and to interpret female crime from a feminist perspective (Flavin, 2001). The two major issues in feminist criminology are thus: (1) Do traditional male-centered theories of crime apply to women? And (2) what explains the universal fact that women are far less likely than men to involve themselves in criminal activity (Price & Sokoloff, 1995)? The first of these issues is known as the generalizability problem, which is the focus of the next chapter. The second issue is known as the gender ratio problem and will be the major focus of the rest of this book.

Chapter 2

The Generalizability Problem

What Is the Problem?

The generalizability problem has been conceptualized as "the quest to find theories that account equally for male and female offending" (Irwin & Chesney-Lind, 2008:839). The implication of this is, of course, that mainstream ("malestream") theories do not equally account for the criminal behavior of both genders. Mainstream criminology has implicitly assumed that what is good for the rooster is also good for the hen. It is undeniable that our major criminological theories have been overwhelmingly formulated, tested, and evaluated based on information gleaned from all male samples while offending by girls and women has been virtually ignored until relatively recently. Although theory testing has tended to include gender as a predictor variable in multivariate models, Chesney-Lind (2006:8) sees this as little more than an "add women and stir" approach. In short, many feminist criminologist maintain that practically all the theoretical concepts (differential association, strain, poverty, disorganized neighborhoods) on which traditional theories are based "are inscribed so deeply by masculinist experience that this approach will prove too restrictive, or at least misleading [if we attempt to apply it to female criminal behavior]" (Daly & Chesney-Lind, 1988:519).

Criminology's concentration on male offending is reasonable given that the crime problem is essentially a male problem, but as feminist criminologists see it, females also commit crimes and traditional theories that purport to explain male offending may not easily "translate" to female offenders. Eileen Leonard (1995) has examined many of the most popular sociological theories of crime causation with an eye to determining if they can be applied to female criminality. She reasoned that theories "should explain not only why certain people are criminal but, by implication, why others are not" (1995:55). In other words, if we can understand why females commit so little crime perhaps we will simultaneously gain insight as to why males commit so much. Leonard's astute observation motivated the writing of this book. I first provide brief synopses of the theories Leonard addresses and follow with her comments about them relevant to their applicability to female criminal behavior. She begins her examination on mainstream criminological theories with Robert Merton's anomie theory.

Anomie

Robert Merton's anomie theory is basically about how individuals respond to conditions said to exist in capitalist societies (especially the United States) where a disjunction exists between cultural goals and structural impediments to achieving them. The cultural goal in the United States for which everyone is supposed to strive is financial success, but the structure of society is such that certain segments of it are denied access to legitimate means of attaining those goals. Most people respond by conforming; i.e., striving to obtain success via legitimate means. Others are ritualists in that they employ legitimate means of making a living but have given up on striving for the "American Dream." Then there are the retreatists who give up on both the goals and the means of attaining them and drift off into alcoholism and/or drug abuse, and the rebels who also reject both the goals and means but want to substitute alternate legitimate goals and means. Finally there are the innovators who accept the financial success goals but reject (or are denied access to) legitimate means of obtaining them in favor of illegitimate (criminal) ways. Criminals in anomie theory are thus deprived persons using criminal means to get what their culture has taught them to want.

Leonard's major criticism of anomie theory is that it is about common success goals supposedly applicable to all members of a capitalist society, and thus does not address gender-specific (or race-, class-, or ethnic-specific) goals. She says that anomie theory cannot be applied to women because women are socialized to be successful in relationships, to get married, and to raise families, not to pursue financial success. The theory does not take into consideration that there is no single cultural success goal for all to strive for; there are two cultural success goals, one for men and one for women. The failure to succeed in either goal is productive of strain, but even if crimes committed by males are innovative means of attaining their *success* goals, it is illogical to view female crimes as innovative means to their *relationship* goals. Anomie is thus very much a male-centered theory since it only addresses the difficulties faced by males in attaining their goals, but Leonard contends that it may become workable for women if their goals shift more toward male-typical goals such as career success.

Subcultural Theories

Subcultural theories add to the insights of anomie theory by indicating how and why subcultures may form among aggregated people who feel the bite of alleged blocked opportunities most sharply. According to subcultural theorists, when a significant number of people feel alienated from the mainstream culture they selectively aggregate and forge a distinctive lifestyle. Members of these subcultures supposedly cannot live up to "middle-class measuring rods," develop "status frustration," and engage in malicious and destructive behavior that Albert Cohen calls "short-run hedonism."

In common with Cohen, Richard Cloward and Lloyd Ohlin's opportunity structure theory maintains that lower-class youths have little interest in pursuing middle-class avenues to success, preferring instead "big cars," "flashy clothes," and "swell dames" (1960:96). However, they make the point that not everyone denied access to legitimate opportunities have access to illegitimate opportunities. Those who have access to illegitimate opportunities through relatives and friends join criminal gangs and commence their "careers"; those who do not join conflict gangs or retreatist gangs. Cloward and Ohlin characterize individuals in these gangs as "double failures" since they have failed in both the legitimate and illegitimate opportunity structures.

Walter Miller's focal concerns theory takes issue with the idea that subcultures are formed in reaction to middle-class status deprivation. He asserted that lower-class culture must be viewed in its own terms, not as a simple negation of middle-class standards. Delinquents and criminals may resent the middle-class, he argued, but this resentment is born not from envy over what they are but from what they have. Components of a middle-class lifestyle such as hard work, responsibility, and reliability are not appealing to them, but what these traits can result in are. Miller identified six focal concerns that are integral to understanding lower-class culture, and thus lower class crime: trouble, toughness, smartness, excitement, fate, and autonomy. Since no one imagines that the middle-class values weakness, dullness, boredom, and being controlled, these things obviously mean different things among the lower-class than they do among the middle-class. In any case, these concerns lead to all kinds of behavior, including criminal behaviors, that perpetuate lower-class subcultures.

Leonard maintains that the subcultural theories of Cohen, Cloward and Ohlin, and Miller are also inadequate explanations of female crime. Unlike Merton, Cohen recognized that males and females have different goals (financial success versus relationship success). Female goals are supposedly easier to achieve, and thus the problems leading to the establishment of delinquent subcultures are fundamentally male problems. Because they cannot measure up to middle-class standards of success and status, boys in delinquent subcultures seek vindication of their male status in delinquent gangs and come to define as meritorious "the characteristics they *do* possess, the kinds of conduct of which they *are* capable" (Cohen, 1955:66; emphasis original). On the other hand, according to Cohen, not only is delinquent gang activity irrelevant to the vindication of a girl's female status, but participation threatens it. For girls, it is "sexual delinquency" that is the typical response to their central concern of establishing a satisfying relationship.

According to Leonard, while Walter Miller's focal concerns theory addresses lower-class culture in general, it is really only a male-centered theory of criminality. His focal concerns are male concerns and have little salience for females and are thus not amenable to considerations of female crime. Leonard contends that if the focal concerns characterized lower-class life in general; i.e., if they were equally salient for males and females in lower-class areas, male and female delinquency and crime rates would be similar. Since they are not, she dismisses the theory as inadequate for explaining female crime. In stating it this way Leonard is implicitly rejecting any explanation for gender differences in criminal behavior other than learned norms and values.

Because Cloward and Ohlin's theory considered the availability of both legitimate and illegitimate opportunities, Leonard sees more hope for it. Cloward and Ohlin stated that women are frequently excluded from delinquent and criminal activities, even within subcultures that support it for males. Thus, not only are females denied full access to the legitimate opportunities of society but also to its illegitimate opportunity structure, and this exclusion could possibly explain women's lower rates of offending. However, Cloward and Ohlin still emphasized common (not gender-related) cultural goals, and their theory cannot explain why women who have achieved their relationship goals commit crimes. Some theorists assert that female crime rises as their participation in the workforce increases, but according to the differential opportunity perspective, the provision of legitimate opportunities is supposed to prevent crime. In short, Leonard concludes that none of the subcultural theories she addressed are of use in explaining female crime.

Differential Association

Differential association theory is a social psychological theory that asserts that crime is learned in intimate personal groups populated by individuals with antisocial behavior and attitudes. How well individuals learn criminal attitudes and behaviors depends on the priority, frequency, duration, and intensity of their associations with such groups. One is more likely to have these associations in lower-class neighborhoods where "definitions" favorable to crime abound. Of course, people learn definitions favorable to law-abiding behavior also, so the key proposition of the theory asserts that crime and delinquency result from an excess of definitions favorable to law violation over definitions unfavorable to law violation learned in intimate personal groups.

Leonard avers that males are more likely than females to attach themselves to groups holding antisocial definitions, and females are more likely to attach themselves to the family, where they will learn fewer definitions favorable to law violation and more favorable to law-abiding behavior. This still begs the question, of course, about why this should be so other than to claim that females are more closely supervised than males. Leonard is more positive toward differential association theory than toward the other theories because it "reminds us that women are not permitted the same associations as men" and that they are taught different things (1995:61). However, she sees the theory as better for explaining why females commit less crime than men, which is the gender ratio problem, rather than as one that is able to explain female crime on its own terms.

Labeling

Labeling theory shifts the focus and the blame for crime away from the offender and onto the criminal justice system. Its main idea is that since (according to the theory) crime has no objective existence but is rather some non-conforming act that is arbitrarily criminalized, searching for causes of crime is a fool's errand. The initial criminalized act is termed primary deviance and could be committed by anyone, but lower-class and minority individuals are more likely to be arrested and thus labeled as delinquents and criminals. Once arrested and labeled, "delinquents" and "criminals" change their self-concepts to conform to the expectations inherent in the label. This change in self-concept leads to secondary deviance (further acts labeled criminal) both because of others' reaction to the stigmatized label and because those labeled come to see themselves as being what they have been labeled.

According to Leonard, one of labeling theory's propositions is that social control agents with the power to apply stigmatizing labels do not associate certain groups with crime. Because traditional stereotypes of women see them as dependent, passive, nurturing, and so forth, they are less likely to be labeled than men. Labeling theorists might posit that women may have crime rates more closely matching those of males than official statistics would have us believe, but because they are not arrested or charged, and thus not officially labeled, they only *appear* to be less involved in primary deviance. Also, not having suffered the stigma of a deviant label, they are not placed at risk for identity change and secondary deviance. Leonard dismisses this as thoroughly rejected by research; i.e., there is widespread agreement that females do indeed commit far less crime than males. She also rejects the entire labeling perspective as lacking an explanation of why people engage in deviance in the first place (recall that labeling theorists are dismissive of what they call "primary deviance" because of their belief that deviance has no objective existence) and because it lacks an analysis of the structures of power and oppression impinging on women.

Marxism

Karl Marx wrote very little about crime, but what little he did write came to be interpreted by his followers as the primitive rebellion hypothesis. Criminal behavior is the behavior of people who are alienated from their work, from others, and from themselves, and who are rebelling against the poverty and oppression of capitalism. The cause of crime is thus quite simple and straightforward for Marxist criminologists—capitalism causes crime and only its overthrow will eliminate it.

Although sympathetic to the Marxist perspective because it focuses on rule making as well as rule breaking, Leonard also criticizes it for its neglect of gender issues. She feels that this perspective is particularly well suited to explore how gender differences interact with class to produce crime, but says that this has not been done. Marxism's emphases on power relations and on the exploitation and oppression of one group by another fits in well with the feminist agenda, but its strict reliance on a class analysis does not allow it to account for female crime. She further maintains that working-class women experience the same capitalist exploitation as working-class men, but they still commit far less crime. Nevertheless, Marxism should resonate well with some of the more radical areas of the feminist agenda. One of the goals of Marxism was to destroy the nuclear family because it viewed as a "bourgeois" property-based notion that exploits women just as the bourgeoisie exploits the proletariat. Marriage was the original class struggle for Friedrich Engels, Marx's long-time collaborator: "The first division of labour is that between man and woman for child breeding ... The first class antagonism which appears in history coincides with the development of the antagonism between man and woman in monogamian marriage" (1884/1988:720).

Female-Centered Theory

We can identify with the frustration evidenced by Jodi Miller's statement that: "applying theories of male crime to women but not theories of women's crime to male offending makes 'women a subcategory of men'" (in Lanier & Stuart, 2010:328), but where are the theories of women's crime that could be applied? Regarding feminists' efforts to build a fully feminist theory of female offending, Jeanne Flavin (2001:273) writes that: "feminist approaches have worked better to criticize than to construct core theoretical frameworks." Many other feminist criminologists have also concluded that male-centered theories have limited applicability to females, but despite their best efforts there is still no female-specific theory of criminal behavior. Some feminist scholars believe that no such theory is possible and that feminist criminologists must be content to focus on crime-specific "mini-theories" that provide "texture, social context, and case histories of women becoming involved in crime" (Daly & Chesney-Lind, 1988:518).

Feminist scholars thus tend to focus more on men's victimization of women and to concentrate on case histories in the tradition of Marxist and conflict theories (Akers & Sellers, 2009). Toward this end, feminist criminologists have developed a series of models cataloging the responses of girls and women to situations more or less specific to their gender that result in them committing *specific* criminal acts rather than crime in general. For instance, a typical female role is that of shopping, and females are arrested for shoplifting (a criminal extension of a traditional female role) more often than males (Smart, 1976). Because women are said to exchange sex for financial security in marriage, some feminists also view prostitution as an illegitimate extension of a legitimate role (Morris, 1987), which is clearly an affront to married women.

Meda Chesney-Lind (1995) combines this "role extension" idea with structural patriarchy to develop a model she calls *criminalizing girls' survival*. She describes a sequence of events related to the efforts of parents and social control agents to closely supervise the lives of girls. She notes that girls are more likely than boys to be reported to the authorities for status offenses such as running away from home or for other status offenses such as being ungovernable, and takes this as evidence that girls are given less behavioral leeway than boys.

Chesney-Lind also notes that girls are more likely to be sexually victimized than boys, that their assailants are more likely to be family members, and that a likely response is to run away from home. The first runaway offense will probably result in the girl being returned to the very conditions she sought to escape. This both reinforces the girl's feelings that "nobody cares" and strengthens her resolve not to get caught again. When a girl is on the streets as a runaway, she has to do something to survive: steal money, food, or clothing; use and sell drugs; and possibly engage in prostitution. These behaviors learned on the streets may then become lifetime patterns of antisocial behavior. Chesney-Lind's point is that girls' victimization and their response to it are shaped by their status in a patriarchal society in which males dominate the family and define their daughters and stepdaughters as sexual property. When girls run away from homes in which they are sexually exploited, they are returned by paternalistic juvenile authorities who feel it is their duty to "protect" them. Thus, patriarchy (as expressed in family dynamics) combines with paternalism (as expressed in official reactions to female runaways) to force girls to live "lives of escaped convicts" (1995:84).

Along the same lines as Chesney-Lind's analysis of criminalizing girls' survival is the concern for explaining female homicide. Homicide is a crime that is mostly *intra*sexual for men but *inter*sexual for women, which suggests that the causes of homicidal behavior might be quite different for men and women. It has been pointed out that in proportional terms African American women are second only to African American men in the frequency of arrest for homicide (Barak, 1998; Mann, 1995). Feminist criminologists have explained this using the concept of *victim-precipitated homicide,* which is a homicide in which the murder victim initiates the sequence of events that leads to his or her death. Most instances of homicide committed by African American females (white female homicide perpetrators also) involve women killing their husbands or boyfriends in self-defense situations (Mann, 1988; Richie, 1996; Serran & Firestone, 2004). Black females may be more reluctant to report battering than white females due to an alleged greater acceptance of violence in the black subculture, and they may be less willing or less able to make use of agencies dealing with spousal abuse (Rasche, 1995). The greater victimization of black women relative to women of other races, as well as barriers preventing their escape from the situation, may lead them to resort to violent solutions to protect themselves more often than other women who presumably have more nonviolent options available to them. The easy availability of guns in American society is also a quite obvious reason why females are able to mount deadly responses to assaultive males.

The Generalizability Problem Is Not a Problem

There is no *uniquely* feminist theory of criminal behavior, nor, in my opinion, should we expect one. Any adequate theory of male criminality should also be adequate to explain female criminality unless we conceive of men and women as two entirely different species. After all, female offenders are over-whelmingly found in the same places as their male counterparts in the social structure; that is, among single-parent families located in poor, socially dis-organized neighborhoods. This was recognized more than three-quarters of a century ago in Sheldon and Eleanor Glueck's *Five Hundred Delinquent Women* (1934). So demographically, at least, theories that address these factors generalize to females. As Bennett, Farrington, and Huesmann (2005:280) put it: "Males and females are not raised apart and exposed to an entirely different set of de-velopmental conditions." Certainly, males and females can be affected to dif-ferent degrees by the same environmental trials and tribulations, but criminogenic risk factors are nonetheless criminogenic risk factors for both males and females (Steffensmeier & Haynie, 2000).

Individual-level correlates of male offending such as low self-control, low IQ, conduct disorder, ADHD, sexual promiscuity, and so forth, are also cor-related with females offending (Moffitt et al., 2001), and again this is something the Gluecks pointed out in 1934. Both genders share the same behavioral reper-toire qualitatively, but they differ quantitatively, as do individuals within each gender. For a whole host of reasons to be address in this book, females are less likely to be affected by the factors that place individuals at risk for antisocial behavior when exposed to them. Gwynn Nettler summarizes these factors under the rubric of greater female "durability": "Environments—good or bad, and whichever facet of them is considered—affect males, the less viable of the sexes more strongly than they do females, the more durable segment of the species" (1982:138).

That men and women respond in similar ways (albeit more or less strongly) to the same environmental factors is driven home by the extraordinarily high correspondence of male and females crime rates. Campbell, Muncer and Bibel (2001:484) report Pearson correlations between male and female violent and property *crime rates* over time in the United States of .95 and .99, respectively. They report almost identical correlations from British data (.98 and .99), and that the average correlations across a number of countries for a variety of crimes are all in the mid to upper .90s. These correlations do not mean, as some people have interpreted them to mean, that males and females have roughly the same incidence (frequency) of offending or prevalence (proportion of each gender offending). What they tell us that no matter how wide the gen-der gap in criminal behavior is across and within nations, when male rates rise, so do female rates, and when male rates fall, so do female rates. As Stef-fensmeier and Allan (1996:465) phrase it: "Statistically when the female rates for a given group are regressed on the males rates for the same group across time and across crime categories, the results for most comparisons do not differ significantly from a prediction of no difference." Thus, large gender differences in criminal offending exist over a wide range of social and cultural conditions even though these conditions affect the crime rates of both sexes/genders similarly in terms of raising or lowering them.

Because male and female crime rates march in lockstep, again indicating that risk factors for males are also risk factors for females, the environmental risk and protective factors proposed by mainstream criminology cannot account for sex *differences* in the incidence and prevalence of offending. In this sense feminists such as Leonard and Chesney-Lind are quite correct. If we are constrained to operate under sociology's strict environmentalist paradigm, which is suspicious of psychological or biological factors that differentiate among individuals and categories of individuals, then these alleged causes should be experienced by males and females similarly, and thus male and female crime incidence and prevalence of offending should be roughly equal. The fact that they are not implies that there is something about gender per se that intervenes between environmental stimulus and behavioral response that is responsible for the different level of offending between males from females. These differences influence the level of environmental instigation required for a person to cross the threshold from law abiding to criminal behavior (Steffensmeier & Haynie, 2000). All evidence points to the fact that when females cross that line they do so at higher thresholds, thus we may argue that there is only one problem worthy of serious pursuit in feminist criminology—why is this so? Asking why it is so is the gender ratio problem.

Chapter 3

The Gender Ratio Problem and Socialization

The Gender Gap in Criminal Offending

Having examined the generalization problem, the task of the remainder of the book is to examine the gender ratio problem. Unlike the generalization problem, which involves a lot of philosophical nit-picking, the gender ratio problem is real and urgent. Bernard, Snipes, and Gerould (2010:299) go so far as to write that the "gender ratio problem may be considered the single most important fact that criminology theories must be able to explain." It may or may not be the most important thing on the criminological agenda, but it certainly is high on the list. The fact of huge gender differences in criminal behavior is not in dispute by feminists or anyone else: "[W]omen have had lower rates of crime in *all nations,* in *all communities* within nations, for *all age groups,* for *all periods in recorded history,* and for practically *all crimes*" (Leonard, 1995:55; emphasis original). Ellis and Walsh (2000:103) surveyed 317 studies from 26 different countries that looked at violent, property, drug, "unspecified" offenses, and delinquency, all of which showed males to be more seriously and frequently involved than females.

Figure 3.1 shows percentages of males and females arrested for seven of the eight FBI index crimes (FBI, 2009) in 2008 (rape is omitted because the 82-fold difference cannot be sensibly graphed without distorting the remaining comparisons). Note that there are about nine males for every one female arrested for murder and robbery, but less than two males for every female arrested for larceny/theft. Thus the more serious, brutal and violent the offense the more males dominate in its commission. For instance, a study of 1,072 gang-related homicides in three cities found that female gang-member committed only eight (0.7%) of them (Sheldon, Tracy & Brown, 2001), and four-year study from Chicago found that only one gang-related homicide out of 345 was committed by a female (Spergel, 1995). The important question is, of course, why this is so. This chapter examines the question from the viewpoints of social constructionist and liberal environmentalist feminist criminologists.

Socialization

Traditional sociology views gender differences (indeed, any differences across any classifications of individuals) in any behavior, aptitude, and attitude as products of differential socialization. From this standpoint, there is nothing biological underlying these different traits despite the fact that behavior genetic studies consistently report medium to large heritability coefficients for all traits, behaviors, and aptitudes (reviewed in Walsh, 2009). Socialization viewed from a sociological lens is Tinbergen's development question uncontaminated by anything so troublesome as genes, brains, hormones, or evolutionary history. Consistent with this view, the higher female threshold for criminal behavior is explained in terms of differential socialization. Males are socialized to be aggressive, dominant, and tough, which are traits conducive to criminal behavior, and females are socialized to be nurturing, empathetic, deferential, and conforming, which are traits conducive to prosocial behavior. This argument suggests that if females were socialized in the same way as males (or vice versa) they would respond to environmental instigations to criminal behavior in like manner and their rates of offending would be roughly the same. This blank slate view was expressed in Leonard's criticism of Walter Miller's focal concern theory noted in the previous chapter when she opined that if lower-class focal concerns were equally salient for males and females there would be no significant differences between delinquency and crime rates between the genders.

The role of socialization cannot be denied as the nurture side of the nature-via-nurture whole. Human beings are exquisitely designed to respond to the environment and to incorporate it into their neural circuitry. This is how we are able to slot into a variety of cultures in ways that could not possibly be prespecified by genes: "The extended period of neuroplasticity [especially during infancy and toddlerhood] is an aspect of human nature that allows and *requires* environmental input for normal human development" (Wexler, 2006:16). The most important environmental input is provided by other human beings who assist the young to adapt to their culture in a continuous process of socialization. Socialization has been defined as the process of internalization "the rules, roles, attitudes, standards, and values across the social, emotional, cognitive, and personal domains" (Grusec & Hastings, 2007:1).

**Figure 3.1 Arrests for FBI Part I Crimes in 2008 by Percentage
Committed by Males and Females (Rape Omitted)**

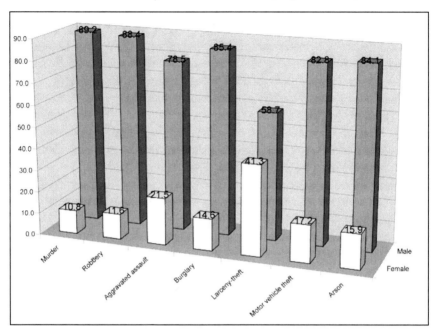

Source: FBI (2009) Crime in the United States: 2008.

As important as the socialization process is, it has been largely conceptualized as a top-down parent-to-child process in which socializers wrote their
scripts on blank slates. Modern developmental researchers realize that children
are not empty vessels that passively receive the stream of proscriptions and
prescriptions being poured into them, and that they are active participants
in the process of becoming social beings. Parents profoundly influence their
children's development, but children's genetic traits and abilities interact with
the traits and abilities of socializing agents in a reciprocal process of mutual
engagement. Children's effects on parents and the role of genes was almost
completely ignored by socialization researchers for most of the 20th century
when more than 99% of socialization studies, according to one estimate
(Plomin, Asbury, & Dunn, 2001), looked at only one child per family. In
order to disentangle genetic from environmental effects and to assess child
effects on parents, researchers need to study more than one child in the same
family. As every parent who has more than one child knows, there are different parenting styles for different children. A parent who is permissive with

a warm and compliant child may be authoritarian with a bad tempered and resistant child, while all the time trying to be an authoritative parent (which psychologists tell us that all parents should be) with both.

Contemporary developmental psychologists now accept the facts that genes influence children's behavior and that parents calibrate their parenting to their children's behavior. Every chapter in the massive and much revered *Handbook of Socialization: Theory and Research* (Grusec & Hastings, 2007) that deals with childhood socialization makes it a point to recognize the important role of genetics (both of the child and its primary socializing agent) in socialization research. Most all contributors to the work are psychologists, however, and psychologists have always been more receptive to the idea that genes influence human behavior than have sociologists. Sociologists hold the tabula rasa view of human nature to a greater extent than psychologists, and have thus been more likely to grant socialization a more powerful and exclusive role in explaining personality, traits, and behavior.[1]

Gender socialization means learning gender behavior, attitudes, and roles considered to be sex-appropriate in one's culture. This learning is imparted from many sources, beginning with the family and is reinforced by friends, school, work, and the mass media. Gender socialization starts at birth because boys and girls are treated differently according to their sex. Parental expectations of boys and girls lead them to buy their children gender-specific toys and assign them gender based tasks. Thus children learn to behave in ways dictated by societal beliefs, values, attitudes, and examples about how boys and girls and men and women ought to present themselves. Children are exposed to norms that define masculine and feminine from an early age. Boys are told not to cry, not to be afraid, and to be assertive and strong. Girls are permitted to cry and are encouraged to be "ladylike." By the time children enroll in school their gender identity is firmly rooted.

The school curriculum reinforces traditional ideas of how girls and boys should act in its course material (Dick and Jane) and activities that separate boys

---

1. In his 2001 Presidential address to the American Sociological Association, Douglas Massey (2002:1) lamented that: "Sociologists have allowed the fact that we are social beings to obscure the biological foundations upon which our behavior ultimately rests." The solution to sociology's problems is for sociologists to learn something about human biology, which might be a necessity for future sociologists. We are seeing more and more statements such as: "If sociologists ignore genes, will other academics—and the wider world—ignore sociology? Some in the discipline are telling their peers just that. With study after study finding that all sorts of personal characteristics are heritable—along with behaviors shaped by those characteristics—a see-no-gene perspective is obsolete" (Shea, 2009:B6).

and girls. These messages are buttressed through interactions with teachers and peers. Teachers are said to reinforce gender roles by encouraging girls to excel in the verbal world and boys to excel at math and science. Teachers are also admonished for differential praising (boys for substantive content and girls for the neatness). Children absorb these lessons and develop an "us and them" attitude, dividing themselves along gender lines in the lunch room and playground. Boys who play with girls are called sissies and perhaps beaten, while girls who play with boys are called tomboys and may be excluded from girls' groups. Peers are thus also powerful socializing agent doling out rewards and punishments and conditioning each other to adopt the "correct" gender attitudes and behaviors.

Children become aware of their sex by about age 2½ and by 3½ they become aware of its stability and that the social world divides people according to male and female (Lippa, 2002). As soon as this awareness strikes them they embark on a subconscious program of self-socialization ("I'm a boy/girl, and this is how I should and will act"). Children soon develop a gender-related self-concept as a boy or girl and seek understanding of what gender behavior is appropriate for them. This is a part of their growing general awareness of how their world is organized and how they and others fit into it. This concept of themselves as male or female is central to children's overall self-concept and is almost impervious to change.

Internalized self-socialization is known as a gender schema theory. The development of this schema is a process by which incoming information is labeled and boxed as male- or female-typed which then becomes the basis for enhanced attention and concern about gender-appropriate behavior on the part of the child. However, cracks began to appear in this theory when a series of longitudinal studies showed that young children preferred to interact with members of their own sex and preferred sex-congruent toys *before* they were able to label behavior or toy preferences, or even correctly sort pictures of girls and boys into appropriate piles (reviewed in Campbell, Shirley, & Candy, 2004; Trautner, 1992). As Campbell (2006:79) put it: "Children seem to need neither the ability to discriminate the sexes nor an understanding of gender stereotypic behavior to show sex differences." Efforts to get children to play with opposite-sex toys or to play in less segregated groups are strongly resisted: "Even when adults try to encourage cross-sex play groups, children resist and quickly return to same-sex partners when adult supervision is reduced" (McIntyre & Edwards, 2009:87). The evidence seems to tell us that what some dismiss as "gender stereotypes" are in fact reasonably accurate assessments of gender differences: Differences lead to stereotypes; stereotypes do not lead to differences.

Early Feminist Theoretical Efforts: Women's Liberation and Crime

The idea that gender is socially constructed, and will change with social changes was expressed in Freda Adler's (1975) *masculinization hypothesis,* which she posited as an explanation for the rise in female crime rates in the 1960s and 1970s. Adler saw this rise as a trajectory that would eventually see a convergence of male and female crime rates. This convergence would occur because an increasing number of females were adopting male roles as the American occupational structure changed by admitting more women. Adler's point was that the adoption of male roles would result in female attitudes and behavior becoming masculinized and would thus eventually commit crimes at rates matching those of males: "In the same way that women are demanding equal opportunity in fields of legitimate endeavor, a similar number of determined women are forcing their way into the world of major crimes" (1975:13). She went on to opine, with apparent relish, that "the status of women in the Mafia may well change," and the reason it may do so is that it cannot ignore the potential competition offered by the "increasing numbers are women [who] are using guns, knives, and wits to establish themselves as full human beings, as capable of violent aggression as any man" (1975:15).

Adler's thesis was not well received by many feminists who did not share her peculiar opinion of how women might establish their humanity, and who also perceived it as providing ammunition for those who oppose women's liberation ("We don't want our women committing crimes or becoming masculinized!"). Other feminists questioned the convergence of male and female rates, with Carol Smart calling it a "statistical illusion caused by the smallness of the [female] base" (1979:53).[2] Pat Carlen (1983:376–377) also strongly criticized Adler's "new female criminal" as essentially a "maladjusted masculininist female" who had rejected her "proper" feminine role, which was an image that differed little from the early commentators on female criminals

---

2. Smart is referring to the fallacy of comparing two sets of percentages with unequal base levels as if they were equal. For instance, suppose in a certain city that females commit 50 homicides in a given year and males commit 500. The following year females commit 65 homicides and males commit 560. The additional 15 female homicides would increase the female rate by 30% while the additional 60 male homicides would only increase to male rate by 12%. Although in terms of absolute numbers male homicides increased four times more than female homicides, in "percentage increase" terms (comparing 30% to 12%) one might get the impression that females were "catching up."

such as Cesare Lombroso, Sigmund Freud, and W. I. Thomas. Finally, Steven Goldberg (1986:30) wittily trashed the convergence hypothesis thus: "A glance at state or federal crime statistics exposes the fact that the girls' rate is increasingly similar to that of boys in the sense that a puddle in an April shower is increasingly similar to an ocean."

Rita Simon (1975) offered a different view, claiming that increased participation in the workforce affords women greater opportunities to commit job-related crime, a position that came to be known as the *emancipation hypothesis*. Taken together, Adler's and Simon's hypotheses have been called the *convergence hypothesis*. Simon noted that women could commit "financial and white-collar crimes," such as "fraud, embezzlement, larceny and forgery" (1975:2), and denied Adler's notion that to engage in crime women would have to become more masculine. She even argued that female violence will decrease rather than increase due to occupational involvement outside of the home. This is because women's "motivation to kill," she said, arises from the exploitation, frustration, and dependency that supposedly comes from the traditional housewife role, and these feelings would be reduced by outside employment. Thus women are quite capable of committing crimes when the opportunity presents itself without first undergoing masculinization. Women's emancipation, while it would generate an increase in non-violent crime, would simultaneously reduce women's violent crime by reducing their frustrations.

Another interpretation linking women's liberation to the increased female crime rates, and one that also implies some degree of rate convergence is the *economic marginalization hypothesis*. This perspective argues that both Adler and Simon neglected to pay sufficient attention to patriarchy and the extent to which it allows males the power to control females' labor and sexuality. Research has suggested that much of female crime is related to economic need, and that women's poverty and crime rates have risen in tandem (Hunnicutt & Broidy, 2004). According to this hypothesis, both the increasing crime and poverty rates are indirectly related to the women's liberation movement. Specifically, the woman's liberation movement has generated efforts by women to free themselves from the power of men, but by doing so they have freed men from their traditional roles as providers. The sexual revolution coupled with the decline in the traditional modes of male respect for women has led to an enormous increase in both out-of-wedlock births and divorce. These things have led to female-headed households and the "feminization of poverty," which motivates women to engage in economically-related crimes such as prostitution, drug sales, and shoplifting (Reckdenwald & Parker, 2008).

That female-headed households are strongly related to poverty is borne out by the U.S. Census Bureau's (2002) breakdown of family types by race and income showing that a black two-parent family is less than half as likely to be poor as a white female-headed single parent family (18.8% versus 41.1%). In other words, white female single-parent households were more than twice as likely as black two-parent households to have an annual income of less than $25,000. These figures constitute powerful evidence that single parenting, whether the result of illegitimacy or family breakup, is a major cause of poverty across all racial lines.

Female-headed households are themselves powerful predictors of delinquent and criminal behavior in a neighborhood. For instance, a study of 264 rural counties in four states by Osgood and Chambers (2003) showed that high rates of population turnover and high levels of ethnic diversity led to social disorganization, but the most important factor predicting crime was high rates of female-headed households. The most notable finding of the study was that "a 10 percent increase in female-headed households was associated with a 73- to 100-percent higher rates of arrest for all offenses except homicide [a 10% increase in female-headed households was associated with a 33% increase in homicide]" (Osgood & Chambers, 2003:6). Of course, it is an open question as to how much of the increase in divorce and children born out-of-wedlock is attributable to the women's liberation movement.

Is the Converge Hypothesis Supported by Research?

The convergence hypothesis has intuitive appeal if we do not take it too far and hypothesize that male and female crime rates may one day be equal. Despite the criticism the convergence hypothesis has received, it would be surprising given the changing roles of women in Western societies if we did not see at least some evidence of convergence. International data have shown that women are from 5 to 50 times less likely to be arrested than males depending on the country (Wilson & Herrnstein, 1985). In general, the arrest ratio is lower in countries that afford females greater levels of equality with men, indicating more criminal opportunities for women in more egalitarian societies. If we take countries as the units of analysis, these data imply that Goldberg's (1986) April puddle can become something of a river if it rains long enough in enough places. However, converging arrest rates can involve changing police practices in shifting cultures of crime control and involve very different crimes.

Female crime in the United States increased from 1960 to 1994, as did male rates. The subsequent decade saw a decrease in both male and female rates (Rennison, 2009), but as a proportion of total arrests the male/female ratio did not vary by more than five percentage points, and the male/female gap has remained essentially unchanged (Campbell, 2009; Steffensmeier et al., 2006). Darrell Steffensmeier and his colleagues (2006) conducted a study pitting the masculinization hypothesis against a policy change hypothesis to account for an observed diminishing ratio of female to male assault arrests documented in the Uniform Crime Reports (UCR). Using data from the UCR and the National Crime Victimization Survey (NCVS) from 1979 to 2003, they noted that the UCR data showed a 60% rise in the percentage of females arrested for simple assault over the period. At first blush this convergence of arrest rates may be considered indicative of female attitude change (masculinization), but the fly in the ointment was that there was no corresponding convergence for murder, robbery, or aggravated assault evident in the UCR data. The alternative hypothesis is that the convergence is a by-product of police policy changes. Most police departments in the United States now have mandatory arrest policies for domestic violence. This has resulted in net-widening to include arrest for minor physical assaults in domestic situations, which reels in women as well as men.

Furthermore, the alleged increase in female violence documented in the UCR was not borne out by NCVS data collected over the same period (i.e., the ratio of female to male assaults fluctuated only randomly). NCVS data are considered more reliable to assess such matters because it is independent of criminal justice policy shifts. Steffensmeier et al (2006) concluded that net-widening policy shifts have elevated the arrest proneness of females who commit physical attacks/threats of marginal seriousness. In other words, women are not becoming more violent; rather official data increasingly mask differences in violent offending by men and women due to policy shifts. If women had become more masculinized, aggressive, and violent, we would have observed significant increases in female arrests for other violent crimes (homicide, robbery, aggravated assault) that have not been subjected to police arrest policy changes, but we have not.

Lauritsen, Heimer, and Lynch (2009) surveyed a larger pool of UCR and NCVS years that suggests that the gender ratio gap has converged somewhat, but that the phenomenon is due in part to larger decreases in male offending than in female offending. They attribute this to the good economy we enjoyed in the 1990s, changes in the illicit drug market, to the "civilizing" effect on males triggered by the increase of women in the workforce, and to the "greater engagement of men in familial roles" (2009:390–391). They might also have included the incapacitation effect of the prison boom in the same decade, which is said to have independently accounted for at least 25% of the decrease (Spelman, 2000; Rosenfeld, 2000). In terms of our concern about the increasing masculinization of women, Lauritsen and her colleagues (2009:385) conclude: "Our finding show that female rates of violent offending have declined over time; clearly a new violent female offender has not emerged."

In the same issue of *Criminology*, Schwartz and her colleagues (2009) argue that the data on the gender gap over the period that NCVS data has been used to supplement UCR data tends to point to more stability than change. They further argue that because of the massive changes in NCVS methodology in 1993, NCVS data will: "tend to inflate female violence estimates and lower male estimates" (2009:403). Schwartz and her colleagues (2009) put this down to nonresponsive individuals in high offending groups being replaced by others in lower offending groups who are willing to be substitute for them. We can tentatively conclude, then, that the gender gap may be closing somewhat for property crimes, but is not likely to close much for violent crimes, particularly the most serious violent crimes.

Chapter 4

General Feminist Theories of Criminal Behavior

Power-Control Theory

Despite the protestations of some that a general feminist theory of criminal behavior is not possible, there have been some attempts to formulate one. Ironically, the two most known theories have been formulated by men—John Hagan's power-control theory and James Messerschmidt's structured action theory. Both of these theories seek to understand the gender gap in criminal offending but have little to do with exploring offense rate convergence. Both theories view delinquent and criminal behavior, and gender differences in those behaviors, as solely a function of socialization.

Hagan's power-control theory is a combination of Marxist and feminist thinking with some conflict and control theory added for good measure. The theory views criminal and delinquent behavior as a function of power, which is a function of social class and control, which is in turn a function of the family. The two variables of power and control are intimately linked because intrafamily relationships are said to reproduce the power relationships parents hold in the workplace. As Hagan (1989:15) puts it: "Family class structure.... derive[s] from the positions these spouses occupy in their work [and family structure] shapes the social reproduction of gender relations and in turn the social distribution of delinquency." Control theories have traditionally viewed the family as a major source of social control, as does Hagan, but they have neglected to consider variations in that control according to gender and family class position, and the inter-relationships among spouses and parents and children. The consideration of these things is the contribution of power-control theory.

Power-control theory maintains that in families where fathers are the sole breadwinner and mothers are housewives and/or have menial jobs, a *patriarchal* family structure is usually the result. This is especially true if the father is in a position of authority at work giving out orders to subordinates and if the mother works outside the home in a job that requires her to take orders from others. In such a family the father's and mother's workplace experiences are reproduced in the family, and child rearing is left primarily to mothers. Thus a patriarchal family is said to be "unbalanced" in favor of the father in terms of power relationships. Patriarchal families, according to Hagan, grant greater freedom to boys because they are being prepared for traditional male roles while daughters are socialized to be feminine, conforming, and domesticated. Sons are encouraged to take risks and to experiment, while daughters are discouraged from these things, particularly the things that are likely to lead to delinquent activity. Because Hagan (1989) views crime and delinquency as adventurous and exciting risk-taking, and since boys are socialized to take risks and girls are not, herein lies the roots of gender differences in offending.

Hagan argues that in more patriarchal families girls most choose to either endure their plight in silence or to escape from "the sexual stratification of social control" (1990:141). To escape, they are likely to "search for deviant role exits" such as running away, suicide ideation, and delinquency. This "escape" activity becomes most prevalent after puberty when adolescents are searching for autonomy regardless of family type, although this search is presumed to be more conflict-ridden between parents and children from patriarchal families because more egalitarian families already allow children of both genders more independence.

The *egalitarian* family develops in the absence of large differences between the work roles of parents and in which the responsibility for child rearing is shared. Power relations in such families are said to be "balanced" as opposed to "unbalanced" in patriarchal families. Egalitarian parents socialize male and female children similarly (girls will have less prosocial "feminine" expectations imposed on them), and both will be subjected to the same level of control. Similarity of treatment will lead to sons and daughters developing similar traits, attitudes, and behaviors, which implies that girls from such families will increase their delinquent involvement. Hagan (1989:158) claims that while there will be large gender differences in delinquency among children from patriarchal families: "egalitarian families will be characterized by smaller gender differences in delinquency." In other words, because egalitarian families are mostly middle-class, middle-class girls are supposedly less closely controlled than lower-class girls and thus they are more likely to commit delinquent and criminal acts. But according to Siegel (1992:270 emphasis added) it is not only middle-class girls who will increase their offending: "Power-control theory, then, implies that middle-class youth of *both sexes* will have higher crime rates than their lower-class peers." This assertion is contrary to all that we know about the relationship between social class and crime, especially serious crime (Walsh,

2011), and the relationship between social class and control of children's behavior (Grusec & Hastings, 2007).

Tests of power-control theory typically ask their subjects about parents' occupations and on that basis assign them into patriarchal or egalitarian family categories. In other words, power-control researchers assume that we can adequately infer the complexity of family dynamics simply by asking about parents' occupations. Other researchers will assign categories to female-headed families (in which there can be no power imbalance) by noting the woman's occupational role. The family will be classified patriarchal if she has no power in the workforce, but egalitarian if she is some sort of supervisor or group leader, no matter how lowly the job (Bates, Bader, & Mencken, 2003). This methodology is almost as arbitrary as classifying the contents of a 100-unit storage facility on the basis of the odd-even numbering dichotomy and underlines the poverty of trying to make sense of complex behavior within a single disciplinary domain. On the other hand, Hagan (1989; 1990) does admit that his theory best "explains" only minor delinquent misbehaviors such as smoking, drinking, and fighting, which leaves unaddressed the serious violent crimes that most strongly differentiate male and female offending.

Structured Action Theory: "Doing Gender"

James Messerschmidt's structured action theory also grants socialization an exclusive role in explaining the gender crime ratio, although its focus is on men and "doing masculinity." Messerschmidt's male focus is not problematic for feminists because "[F]eminist inquiry is not limited to topics about women, it focuses on men as well" (Daley & Chesney-Lind, 1988:503). Central to this theory is the concept of *hegemonic masculinity,* which is the cultural ideal of masculinity that men are expected to live up to. Hegemonic masculinity is "defined through work in the paid-labor market, the subordination of women, heterosexism, and the driven uncontrollable sexuality of men" (Messerschmidt, 1993:82). This is not necessarily the most prevalent expression of masculinity in any culture or subculture because the bar is set high, but rather it is the most socially endorsed. Although it is about living up to masculine ideals and distancing the masculine self from femininity, it is also a way to maintain patriarchy (Connell & Messerschmidt, 2005), and implies that reduced patriarchy may result in gender offending convergence.

According to Messerschmidt, gender is not something imposed on a person, or what one is; rather, gender is something one demonstrates and accomplishes. He is concerned with how men "do gender." Doing gender is an ongoing dynamic process by which males express their masculinity to audiences of men and women so that it may be socially validated. This expression can take many forms according to culture and social context which jointly informs males of the appropriate norms of masculine behavior. To project a positive masculine image to the world, a man must learn the relevant cultural and subcultural definitions of masculinity via socialization. Traditional middle-class ways of doing masculinity (proving one's manhood) include being successful in a career, having and providing for a wife and children, being a good protector, and projecting an aura of quiet dominance as well as physical and mental strength.

When males cannot or will not strive to accomplish legitimate modes of doing gender they develop alternative modes to accomplish the same result, which are often criminal in nature. Being tough and courageous is central to a masculine identity in all social classes, although they mean different things in different classes, cultures and subcultures, and among different races. In lower-class cultures this often involves violent confrontations over status issues because taking matters into ones own hands is seen as the only way to obtain "juice" (masculine status) on the street (Anderson, 1999). These violent confrontations are generally the result of trivial altercations over matters of honor, respect, and reputation ("dissing" one's masculinity), and tend to take place in front of an audience so that the maximum amount of "juice" is squeezed from the incident (Buss, 2005; Mazur & Booth, 1998). Violent and criminal behavior can thus be used as a resource for accomplishing masculinity—"doing gender."

Messerschmidt also theorizes about "doing femininity" among gang girls and women engaging in "bad girl femininity." Although violence is defined culturally as masculine behavior, Messerschmidt (2002:465) asserts that if females engage in it they are "not attempting increasingly to be masculine, but, rather, were engaging in physical violence authentically as girls and as a legitimate aspect of their femininity." Violent gang females do not consider themselves masculine, then, but rather as "bad." Gang girls are emphatic about their feminine identity and are "very fussy over gender display (clothes, hair, makeup) and, thus, for the most part display themselves as feminine in 'culturally approved' ways" (Messerschmidt, 2002:464).

Messerschmidt wants to show that because gender is fluid and context specific there is no incompatibility between "acting bad" and femininity. Girls and women fight to defend friends, the "hood," and "her man" from the poaching efforts of other females. He also wants to emphasize that the construction of a "bad ass" image is not a constant concern for gang females as it is among gang males, and that it is very much subordinate to constructing a feminine image. When females fight, they are contextually "doing masculinity" just as males contextually "do femininity" when "comforting and nurturing a fellow gang member" (2002:473).

By emphasizing the lengths that males and females will go to maintain and validate their self-images as masculine and feminine across a wide range of cultural and situational domains, Messerschmidt is (inadvertently) pointing to something deeper than socialization. Contrary to his assertion that gender is "not what one is," surely "doing gender" an affirmation of a core identity that is indeed "imposed on" males and females by their biological sex. Certainly *how* one affirms and validates this core identity depends on culture, learning, and on the situation, but the *motivation* to do so is an unlearned crosscultural constant. Additionally, much of Messerschmidt's work is a restatement of the male concerns identified by the old subcultural theories regarding status competitions in chaotic neighborhoods.

Gender Differences Explained by Gender-Differentiated Traits

The work of Mears, Ploeger, and Warr (1998) provide us with an example of explaining gender differences in antisocial behavior by appealing to behavioral traits that are quantitatively different among males and females. Their position is that the genders differ in criminal behavior because they differ in exposure to delinquent peers, and because males are more likely to be affected by delinquent peers than females. They assert that females are less likely to be so affected because females have a greater sense of morality, greater empathy, and different cognitive skills which exert a strong inhibitory affect on their behavior. This is correct, but there is little substance in them beyond stating in a roundabout way that "boys will be boys," and "girls will be girls." What we would like to know is *why* males are more likely to be exposed (or to expose themselves) to delinquent peers and *why* they are more affected by them once they are exposed. We should also like to know *why* females have greater empathy, a greater sense of inhibitory morality, and different cognitive skills.

Predictably, Mears, Ploeger, and Warr couch their explanations of these things in terms of gender role socialization. They tell us that females are not as likely to be exposed to delinquent peers because they are more strictly supervised, and they are more morally inhibited because they are socialized more strongly to conformity. Similarly, Heimer and De Coster (1999:306) maintain that "boys are more violent than girls largely because they are taught more definitions favoring such behavior; girls are less violent than boys because they are controlled through subtle mechanisms, which include that violence is incompatible with the meaning of gender for them." The way children are socialized and supervised certainly impacts decisions to misbehave for both genders, but controlling for supervision level results in the same large gender gap in offending; that is, comparably supervised boys have higher rates of delinquency than girls (Gottfredson & Hirschi, 1990). Further adding to the misery of this position is a meta-analysis of 172 studies that found a slight tendency for boys to be *more* strictly supervised than girls (Lytton & Romney, 1991).

Another surprising finding from Lytton and Romney's meta-analysis was how few parent-initiated (as opposed to child-initiated) behaviors and socialization patterns were gender differentiated. One gender-differentiated behavior was that parents displayed more warmth to girls than to boys, the obvious explanation for which is that parental warmth is an evoked response to the greater warmth girls displayed toward their parents. This is known as evocative gene-environment correlation (rGE) in behavior genetics.[1] Subsequent studies have shown that large sex differences in antisocial behavior exist regardless of level of supervision and whether or not the family is patriarchal or egalitarian (Chesney-Lind & Shelden, 1992).

Evaluating Socialization as the Cause of Gender Differences

Family socialization of the kind stressed by the theorists in this chapter is an example of what behavior geneticists call *shared environmental effects*. When

---

1. The rGE concept means that genotypes and the environments they find themselves in are not random with respect to one another. Parents provide their offspring with genes for traits and environments conducive to their expression. This is known as *passive rGE*. *Evocative rGE* refers to the way parents, siblings, teachers, peers, and all others in the social environment react to the individual on the basis of his or her evocative behavior. The treatment of children by others is as much a function of children's evocative behavior as it is of the interaction style of those who respond to them. Children bring traits with them that increase or decrease the probability of evoking certain kinds of responses when they interact with others. *Active rGE* refers to individuals actively seeking environments compatible with their genetic dispositions. Within the range of cultural possibilities and constraints, genes help to determine what features of the environment will and will not be salient and rewarding. The constant interplay between genes and environments informs us of how what may initially be a small genetic effect snowballs into large phenotypic effect as individuals select and create environments compatible with their genetic propensities and as others react to them on the same basis (Cary, 2003).

behavior geneticists study phenotypic traits they decompose variance into genetic, shared environmental and non-shared environmental effects. Shared environment refers to the environment experienced by children reared in the same family, and include such variables as parental SES, religion, values and attitudes, parenting style, family size, intactness of home, and neighborhood. Non-shared environment can be familial or extra-familial. Familial non-shared variables include gender, birth order, perinatal trauma, illness, and parental favoritism. Extra-familial non-shared factors include experiences unique to the individual such as having different peer groups and teachers. Behavior genetic studies do not typically endeavor to determine what those factors are; they leave that to the social scientists.

Shared environments are assumed to make people alike just as shared genes are assumed to make same-sex individuals alike. It is consistently found that while shared environmental effects have considerable similar effects on siblings' personalities and cognitive abilities during childhood, these effects fade to almost nothing in adulthood. In other words, the similarity of socialization experiences of siblings reared in the same household make them similar on many phenotypic measures while they live together, but they fail to survive into adulthood (Bouchard, 2004). As we grow older genetic factors and non-shared environmental factors become more salient. Gendered behavior is a function of how we think and feel about ourselves and an integral part of our personalities, and since shared environmental effects on personality do not survive into adulthood, we gift the influence of parental socialization too much for the development of gender differences in personality, identity, and behavior.[2]

Heaping further agony on socialization to explain gender differences are a number of large cross-cultural studies conducted during the first decade of the 21st century. Recall that the convergence hypothesis discussed in Chapter 3 relies on a social role model that predicts gender differences in personality and behavior will diminish as the sexes come to occupy similar social roles in more egalitarian and less patriarchal cultures (Wood & Eagly, 2002). Sex role theory would therefore predict that gender differences should be strongest in more traditional and patriarchal cultures where sex roles are most distinct. Costa, Terracciano, and McCrae's (2001) study of gender differences in personality across 26 cultures (n = 23,031) showed across all cultures that gender differences were most pronounced in modern *egalitarian* cultures in which traditional sex roles

---

2. This means only that shared environments have minimal to zero effect on sibling *similarity*, not that they have no effect at all. Indeed, the shared environment can have strong effects in opposite directions depending on different sibling genotypes (gene-environment interaction).

are minimized. Another study (McCrae & Tarracciano, 2005) using different measures and 50 cultures (n = 11,985) found exactly the same thing. A study by Schmitt and colleagues (2008) of 55 cultures (n = 17,637) of gender differences using the Big Five personality traits once again found the exact same pattern; i.e., the biggest gender differences were found in cultures where sex role differences are minimized.[3]

While these findings are the direct opposite of what sex role theory predicts, biosocial theorists are not surprised. They fit with all behavior genetic studies of all kinds of traits that show as the environment becomes more equal for the trait in question the more innate (genetic) factors contribute to variance in the trait (heritability coefficients will be higher). Because there are only two sources of trait variance—genetic and environmental—the more one source is equalized the more the influences of the other stand out. This is a simple mathematical truism. Another way of looking at it is to say that in less constraining environments such as those of North America and Western Europe, individuals are freer to be themselves; that is, to live, act, and construct their environments in ways consistent with their genetic proclivities. Thus the increased sexual dimorphism in personality in developed Western societies is simply a function of the natural tendency of males and females to develop different personalities. Schmitt and his colleagues (2008) maintain that traditional agrarian cultures with their typically extreme levels of resources inequalities and gender inequality may represent the largest departure from the egalitarian hunter-gatherer cultures that characterized our species for more than 99.9% of its history. Western post-agrarian cultures are closer to our egalitarian hunter-gatherer psychology (Adkins & Guo, 2008).

Bringing Biology In

Having taken an admittedly brief look at the idea that gender differences in criminal offending is the result of gender differences in socialization, what can we conclude? Dianna Fishbein (1992:100) arrived at her conclusion some time ago: "Cross cultural studies do not support the prominent role of structural and cultural influences of gender-specific crime rates as the type and extent of male

---

3. There are numerous personality traits that have been identified, but modern psychology has boiled most of these diverse traits down to five broad categories known as the Big Five. These five personality traits are derived from factor analyses in which a number of specific traits cluster together into broad categories. These five factors are Openness (to experience), Conscientiousness, Extraversion, Agreeableness, and Neuroticism.

versus female crime remains consistent across cultures." Parents in all cultures socialize males and females differently because they *are* different—the biological dog wags the cultural tail. Socialization patterns, Sanderson (2001:198) insists: "simply represent social confirmation of a basic biological reality that is easily recognized by people in all societies."

Because the gender gap is found across time and cultures, it is a constant, and just as we cannot explain a variable by a constant, we cannot explain a constant by a variable. The invariance of the gender gap must be explained by something which itself is invariant, which socializing practices are not. The invariant is sex-specific developmental physiology undergirded by sex-specific evolutionary pressures. We cannot continue to infer the power of gender-differentiated norms from the gender-differentiated behavior that these norms supposedly explain. Richard Udry (1994:563) calls such reasoning circular, and states: "The reason for this tautology is that we, as social scientists, can't think of any other way to explain sex differences."

Sociologist Alice Rossi could certainly think of other ways. In her 1984 presidential address to the American Sociological Association, she warned her colleagues that if they continued to rely on disembodied phenomena to explain sex/gender differences they would become irrelevant in the scientific world:

> Gender differentiation is not simply a function of socialization, capitalist production, or patriarchy. It is grounded in a sex dimorphism that serves the fundamental purpose of reproducing the species. Hence, sociological units of analysis such as roles, groups, networks, and classes divert attention from the fact that the subjects of our work are male and female animals with genes, glands, bones and flesh occupying an ecological niche of a particular kind in a tiny fragment of time. And human sexual dimorphism emerged from a long prehistory of mammalian and primate evolution. Theories that neglect these characteristics of sex and gender carry a high risk of eventual irrelevance against the mounting evidence of sexual dimorphism from the biological and neurosciences (1984:1).

Rossi is no tool of the patriarchy. She is a card-carrying liberal with impeccable feminist credentials as a founding member of the National Organization of Women! She was simply pointing out that gender differences have arisen out of the fundamentally different reproductive roles males and females play that have been fine-tuned by eons of evolutionary selection pressure. She was also stressing that sociologists must integrate the hard data from the more basic sciences into their work if they and their theories are to attain credibility within the broader scientific community.

Rossi's message and her feminist credentials suggest that there is nothing in biology that is intrinsically incompatible with feminism. Indeed, feminist criminologists would benefit from biosocial explanations of their major issues more than criminologists from other theoretical tradition because of the huge amount of scientific work on sex/gender differences conducted in the robust sciences of genetics, endocrinology, neurobiology, and evolutionary biology. Many other female scientists who identify themselves politically as feminists such as Anne Campbell, Helen Cronin, Diane Fishbein, Patricia Gowaty, Rosemary Hopcroft, Sarah Hrdy, Joan Huber, Linda Mealey, Terrie Moffitt, Barbara Smuts, and Griet Vandermassen, to name just a few who come immediately to mind, are leading figures in biosocial science.

Chapter 5

Social Constructionism and Social Science's Triad of "Evils"

Social Constructionism

This chapter examines social constructionism and the philosophical positions that strict constructionists find insufferable. An examination of the rivalry between social constructionism and its adversaries is important, not only to feminist criminology but to social science in general. I first discuss social constructivism and then turn to how social constructionists view three concepts that I have termed the triad of social science evils—determinism, essentialism, and reductionism. In calling these philosophical positions "evils" I mean that social science references to them are overwhelmingly derogatory and that those espousing them are considered not only wrong (which is forgivable) but malevolently wrong (which is not). Participants in the debates about such things so often misunderstand one another and define their opponents' positions in ways their opponents do not recognize, thus they tend to argue more past one another than with one another.

Every discipline has its own ontology defining the fundamental categories of reality (the assumptions it holds to be "true") within its domain. Each discipline also has its own epistemology that defines how its practitioners know and reason about the reality they assert. Simply put, ontology is the biologist asserting that this animal specimen *is* female; epistemology is the philosopher asking *how* the biologist knows it is female. The biologist will reply by explaining the methods by which biology categorizes sex and describing the things that differentiate one sex from the other. He or she will concentrate on those distinctions that are necessary to placing the specimen into one category versus the other, such as chromosomal and gonadal status. Social constructionism, however, does not admit of any ontological reality, nor is it an epistemology in the sense that it has a set of techniques that allows it to know with universal satisfaction what it alleges, although it certainly has its opinions about the nature of knowledge.

Social constructionism is an approach to knowledge that contends that our realities are created socially by common agreement rather than representing things that "necessarily" exist outside the human understanding of them. We are all social constructionists in the sense that our reality is constructed from common experiences and communally validated. This does not mean that constructionists think that all reality is arbitrary and that brute facts such as chemical elements, disease, and mountains only exist in our collective minds, although sometimes strong social constructionists skid dangerously in this quasi-solipsistic direction. One often gets the impression when reading strong constructionists that they do think that many things are called into existence simply by naming them. However, what constructionists of the weaker variety actually mean is that our *beliefs* about those things and how we respond to them are the result of shared social discourse. It is of course trivially true that we could think about brute facts and react to them in ways other than we do.[1]

We can all agree that at one level *everything* is socially constructed. Because nature does not reveal herself to us ready sorted and labeled, humans must do it for her. Social construction means that humans have perceived a phenomenon, named it, and categorized it according to some taxonomical rule (also

---

1. There some things made real in some sense simply by naming them, such as witches. Witches, at least the broom-riding, spell casting variety, do not exist. But as all sociologists know, if we define something as real it is real in its consequences. Those defined as witches who were burned at the stake took no comfort from their knowledge that they were innocent of practicing the dark arts. However, it is a long way between the medieval authorities defining arbitrary constructs such as witches into existence and modern radical constructionists defining scientific concepts for which there is abundant evidence out of existence.

An example of the value of weak social constructionism is the definition and treatment of homosexual behavior across the centuries. Throughout most of European history same-sex sex was considered a sin to be dealt with by the ecclesiastical courts rather than a crime, although from time to time this was punctuated with secular interference and criminalized. In general, people who engaged in homoerotic behavior were not seen as a special class of people, but rather as individuals who engaged in "unnatural acts." It was not until 1869 that the term "homosexual" was coined, which marked the beginning of the focus on the actors (homosexuals) rather than the act (sodomy). With the coining of the term and with the classification of people into it, legal statutes began to equate all sodomitic sex with homosexuality. As Chauncey and his colleagues (2005:10) assert: "Only in the late nineteenth century did the idea of the homosexual as a distinct category of person emerge, and only in the twentieth century did the state begin to classify and penalize citizens on the basis of their status as homosexuals." Thus, how we define and think about people as a society impacts how we react to it.

socially constructed) that takes note of similarities and differences among the things being classified. Just because something is *necessarily* socially constructed in this sense, it does not mean that the process of categorization is arbitrary and without empirical referents and meaning, as many who try to "deconstruct" concepts they dislike aver. There are problems with our social science constructs, but then very few concepts in any domain of knowledge, with the possible exception of mathematics, are defined and understood in such a way as to make every application of their descriptors unproblematic.

I do not dismiss the value of social constructionism, the real value of which is that it gives us pause when we start to believe that our social practices are natural and inevitable rather than contingent. However, it is surely not a useful epistemology to guide us in our search for knowledge. Social constructionism is a brake preventing us from going too far in our claims rather than an engine moving us forward. In many ways it is a dangerous relativism when it pushes on the brake too hard and diminishes the importance of science in the minds of those too enamored of it. For instance, it has been argued that schizophrenia, as well as certain other mental disorders, is a social construct and thus searching for biochemical causes is futile (Boyle, 1990). We would indeed have given up the search if we came to believe that such disorders had no reality to them beyond psychiatric consensus, but thankfully for those who suffer them we did not. These disorders have identifiable causes and can be treated with medications that we would not have had we succumbed to the social construction argument. Mental disabilities of various kinds have been conceptualized differently at different times and in different places, but do we want to go back to the days when "cold mothers" were cruelly blamed for so many of the syndromes that we now know have real biological referents?

Determinism

Characterizing determinism as "malestream," Bilal Shah (2009:1) writes that: "Determinism and Feminism are as antithetical to each other as sugar is to spice, fire to water, and day to night. Determinism implies that human action is determined by forces independent of will. Feminism implies that structuring of production, reproduction, sexuality and socialization which have put women at a disadvantage can be deconstructed by collective will." Of course, determinism cannot be "malestream" because it cannot be owned by either sex. Determinism is a position relating to how the world is said to operate and is a position held by all scientists, male or female. When scientists speak of determinism they simply mean that every event stands in some causal relationship to other events; that the world is not all chaos and randomness. Surely we are all determinists in this sense. Determinism does not mean that humans cannot change the course of future events, particularly events in their own lives. To assert that they cannot would be fatalism, not determinism, a position it would seem that Shah and others like her apparently confuse with determinism.

When social scientists use the term determinism they are typically thinking of "biological determinism"; cultural determinism is apparently perfectly acceptable. Biological determinism is seen as implying that social behavior is a *direct* outcome of genetic programming absent any influence from the environment. Indeed, feminists' insistence on the sex/gender distinction has its origins as a counter to "biological determinism" because they "knew" that biology is destiny (Mikkola, 2008). Colin Trudge (1999:96) asserts that such accusations represent either mere rhetoric or simple ignorance: "For a start, no evolutionary psychologist [or geneticist or neuroscientist] doubts that a gene is in constant dialogue with its surroundings, which include the other genes in the genome, the rest of the organism, and the world at large." If only those who made accusations of "biological determinism" would learn something about human biology they would not embarrass themselves with such pronouncements.

An additional concern for many social scientists is that explanations of human behavior are socially dangerous if there is even a whiff of biology attached to them. Notwithstanding the fact that there is no such animal as a strictly biological explanation for social behavior, far more damage has been done by a blank slate view of human nature. The environmental determinism implied by such a view is a more sinister form of determinism. Stalin, Mao, Pol Pot, and others of similar mind set, murdered in excess of 100 million people in their belief that they could take empty organisms and turn them into the "new Soviet, Chinese, or Cambodian man" (van den Berghe, 1990:179). A view of human nature that sees each person as a unique individual born with a suite of biological traits with which to interact with the world is more scientifically defensible and respectful of human dignity than tabula rasa views that delight political megalomaniacs who believe that humans can be molded into beings that conform to their vision of social perfection.

Matt Ridley (2003:6) had something quite astute to say about the typical social scientist's fears about genes and "genetic determinism" and why they should rid themselves of such fears:

> Genes are not puppet masters, nor blueprints. They may direct the construction of the body and brain in the womb, but they set about

dismantling and rebuilding what they have made almost at once in response to experience. They are both the cause and consequence of our actions. Somehow the adherents of the "nurture" side of the argument have scared themselves silly at the power and inevitability of genes, and missed the greatest lesson of all: the genes are on our side.

Ridley is saying that genes are at our beck and call; we are not at theirs. Genes are constantly responding to our needs by making the hormones, neurotransmitter, and cell-structure proteins we need as we meet the many challenges of our environments. In contrast to what many social scientists believe about genes, Badcock (2000:71) goes so far as to assert that our genes "positively guarantee" human freedom and agency. If they incline us in one direction rather than another we are being nudged internally, not by something wholly outside of our beings; after all, our genes are *our* genes. Likewise, because so many things that we do in life affects the expression of our genes, epigenetic researcher Randy Jirtle asserts that: "Epigenetics introduces the concept of free will into our idea of genetics" (in Watters, 2006:34).[2] And finally along the same lines, the physicist Steven Rose, who is very much an avocational behavioral scientist, writes: "Individually and collectively we have the ability to construct our own futures, albeit in circumstances not of our own choosing. Thus it is that our *biology* makes us free" (2001:6; emphasis added). Very few social scientists would feel as comfortable making such bold pronouncements about free will and agency as are these natural scientists.

It is true that traits and behaviors imputed to women and considered biologically natural have been used to oppress women in the past, and many feminists believe that modern biology can be used for the same purpose. Biological findings can be used by misogynists to denigrate and oppress women only if we allow them to, and only if we do not counter the ignorance that underpins their arguments. The feminist pursuit of social justice is a *moral* imperative regardless of what science does or does not have to say about any observed differences between the sexes/genders. Science must be our unfettered guide to understanding human behavior because it is about what empirically *is*, not what morally *ought* to be. Justice does not rest on sameness or on differences between the sexes, but on law and reasoned discourse.

---

2. Epigenetics means "in addition" to the genes and is "any process that alters gene activity without changing the DNA sequence" (Weinhold, 2006:163). Epigenetic modification of DNA mean that genes are switched on and off by signals from the internal chemical environment and/or by the external environment according to the needs of the organism. The epigenetics of gene expression may have as much or more influence on the development of individual differences than DNA polymorphisms (Kramer, 2005).

Essentialism

Wood and Eagly (2002:700) define essentialism in a way that I can accept: "Essentialist perspectives emphasize the basic, stable sex differences that arise from causes that are inherent in the human species such as biologically-based evolved psychological dispositions." But this is a more benign definition than what gender feminists have in mind when they accuse someone of essentialism. What they tend to have in mind is the Aristotelian notion that things have "essences" that are necessary and indispensable to them; i.e., essential. An essential property is a property of an object or subject which, if lacking that property, the object or subject cannot be what it is alleged to be. For instance, it is essential that a molecule of water have two hydrogen atoms and one oxygen atom, without either we do not have that molecule of water. Likewise, we can say that it is essential to being male that a person has testes and an XY karyotype, and that it is essential to the being female that a person has an XX karyotype and ovaries, which is an essentialist position according to Wood and Eagly's definition. However, we cannot say that chromosomal or gonadal status is always and unequivocally associated with gender (or even sex, since some individuals have their gonads removed for medical reasons) in the same way that the combination of hydrogen and oxygen are to water. We shall see that a person can be "sexed" a male yet "gendered" a female, but it is surely not a scientific sin to define sex according to these criteria, or even to say they are essential, since it is true in all but the rarest of circumstances.

This observation is merely stating generalities, a practice that many gender feminists apparently view as essentialists and abhor (Barrett, 2001). For instance, in providing an example of her vision of essentialism (which to most other people would be a simple generality), Janis Bohan (1993:7) states that: "If 'friendly' were gendered, an essentialist position might argue that women are more friendly than men ... and the quality is now a trait of women." She goes on to assert that this kind of generalizing is grounded on "problematic universalizing assumptions" that portray women "as a homogeneous class" that fails "to acknowledge diversity among us" (1993:8).

Again, I can understand why feminists might have a problem with essentialism, even if it confused with generalizing, because older "essentialists" attributed essential properties to women (weak, emotional, dull-witted) that were less than flattering and kept them out of the political and occupational arenas and subordinate to men in all arenas. However, in their battle against false generalities anti-essentialist feminists have dismissed all generalities to affirm the existence of nothing but context-specific differences. Considering that feminist criminologists identify the gender ratio as its major concern, we might ask why this is not attacked as essentialist. After all, it asks why men are more antiso-cial at all times and in all places than women. Surely we all recognize that when we make such statements, it is a given that there are individual exceptions to the rule without having to make it explicit.

If feminists such as Bohan define essentialism as the process of generalizing, they are rejecting nomothetic science in favor of idiographic accounts of con-tingent and subjective phenomena. Idiographic accounts have their place, but that is on the therapist's couch or the biographer's word processor where in both places the focus is rightly on the individual. While it is true that each in-dividual has a unique psychological structure, all science tells us that n = 1 is bogus for advancing our knowledge of humankind or anything else. Having no wish to essentialize feminists, let me say that there are many (perhaps most) feminists who are devoted to empirical science (some of the more famous were identified in the previous chapter), even the kinds of science labeled biologi-cal determinism, essentialist, and reductionist by other feminists. I believe that for the most part the charge of essentialism is so much metaphysical waffle be-cause Aristotelian essentialism really did mean invariant, and surely not even the most radical feminist constructionist believes that there is anyone who thinks that anything in the social world is invariant. Nonetheless, the term is useful to reinforce other hissing suffixes such as sexist, fascist, racist, or clas-sist, so beloved by some to stifle inquiry and to congratulate themselves for not belonging to any of those nasty categories.

Reductionism

According to some accounts: "A reductionist theory is a theory that attempts to explain social 'reality' in terms of a single, unifying principle such as 'patriarchy'" (Owen, 2006:900). Theories that qualify as reductionist in this sense are strong versions of feminism (all the woes of women are the result of patriarchy) and Marx-ism (all the woes of everybody are the result of capitalism). If this is reduction-ism, then I repudiate it absolutely. The reductionism that most social scientists abhor is not this, however, but rather the process of examining a complex phe-nomenon at a more basic level. While it is really nothing more sinister to re-ductionism than this, sociologists recoil in horror at the "r word" as if their whole enterprise would explode if they stooped to reducing "social facts" to something more elementary. Reductionists do not suggest that the social factist paradigm be taken back to the drawing board and revamped. They fully realize that while social facts are not readily observable, like gravity their effects are real and are revealed in the enabling and constraining effects they have on human action.

Antireductionists do not recognize the value of reductionism, as is apparent by James Coleman's assertion that when two or more individuals interact: "the *essential* requirement is that the explanatory focus be on the system as a unit, not on the individuals or other components which make it up" (cited in Wilson, 1998:187; emphasis added). This stance is one of strong methodological holism declaring that social facts *must not* be reduced to individual psychology or biology. It is true that the interaction of elements (whether they be chemicals, people, or whatever) produce effects that can be explained on their own terms, but the claim that it is *essential* to focus explanatory efforts only on the whole unit to the exclusion of the parts is unnecessarily constraining. E. O. Wilson (1998:187) pointed out in response to Coleman's position that biology "would have remained stuck around 1850 with such a flat perspective" if it had taken seriously the claim that "the essential requirement is that the explanatory focus be on the organism as a unit, not on the cell or molecules which make it up."

As Wilson implies, cell biologists know that at bottom they are dealing with atomic particles and seek to understand their properties. But as Coleman might stress, they also know that there are properties of the cell that cannot be deduced from those particles *a priori*, that they require functional explanations of the whole cell, and how that cell fits into a network of other cells to form the organism. Thus we need both holistic and reductionist accounts that complement one another rather than exclude. Science is eclectic by nature, and can pose questions and offer explanation at several levels of understanding. Natural scientists have long recognized the complementarity of reductionist and holistic explanations, and useful observations and hypotheses now go in both reductionist and emergent directions in those sciences.

Thomas Nagel, the doyen of the philosophy of science, has pointed out that: "non-reductionist accounts simply *describe* phenomena and reductionist accounts *explain* them" (in Rose, 1999:915). Social scientists who study broad categories of people do not typically turn their attention toward lower levels of analysis when they have identified categories associated with the problem with which they are concerned. They look to variables such as class, gender, patriarchy, capitalism, and so forth, to "explain" behavior, forgetting that such variables are descriptors that beg a multitude of questions rather than explanations. Ceasing the search for explanations with social facts may be true to Durkheim's dictum, but it is poor science. As Lubinski and Humphreys (1997:177) suggest: "Whatever the causes of group differences in social phenomena are, measures of individual differences typically reflect those causes more effectively than does membership in demographic groups." What Lubinski and Humphreys are saying is that lumping everyone into categories such as class or gender, although often useful (dare I say it?), essentializes the members of those categories; i.e., treats them all as essentially alike.

There are certainly times when non-reductionist accounts are more coherent and satisfying than reductionist ones, and we must be careful that we do not lose *meaning* as an essential component to understanding behavior by an overemphasis on mechanisms. Phenomena may be *explained* by lower-level mechanisms, but they find their *significance* in more holistic regions. Propositions about entities such as genes, hormones, and neurons do not contain terms that define the human condition at its most meaningful level. We must not confuse a part, however well we understand it, for the whole. I would condemn Dennett's (1995:82) "greedy reductionist" (a person who skips over several layers of higher complexity in a rush to fasten everything securely to a supposedly solid foundation) just as surely as I would a naive antireductionist who "yearns for skyhooks" (Dennnet, 1995:82). The reductionist point is that science has made its greatest strides when it has picked apart wholes to examine the parts, and in doing so has gained a better understanding of the wholes they constitute. As the heavyweight champion of nature *via* nurture, Matt Ridley (2003:163) has opined: "Reductionism takes nothing from the whole; it adds new layers of wonder to the experience."

Chapter 6

Social Constructionism and Gender

The Social Construction of Gender?

The social constructionist argument is that gender differences are real only to the extent that the majority of people in society believe them to be. For them gender has no logic by which we could predict patterns of behavior from the chromosomal status of individuals across space and time. Unlike sex differences that exist independently of our ideas about them, the existence of gender differences depends on a shared discourse of a particular culture at a particular time and may be, and some of the more radical constructionists insist are, independent of biological sex. For the less radical constructionist, sex differences are like the differences between chemical elements which define their identity at all times and all places and are objective and essential. Gender appropriate behaviors, activities, and mannerisms, on the other hand, are more like clothing, food, or musical fashions that flit in and out of favor fairly arbitrarily across different cultures subcultures and historical periods.

As mentioned above, some social constructionist feminists even claim that sex differences are social constructions. Judith Lorber (1994:46), for instance, wrote that "a purely biological substrate [of gender] cannot be isolated because human physiology is socially constructed and gendered." The best response I can think of to this gem of wisdom was made by Lopreato and Crippen (1999:143) when they wrote: "One wonders whether members of the medical profession are aware of this extraordinary discovery." Other feminists have maintained that such things as pregnancy sickness and menstruation pains are socially constructed, and that because females are fed less and have fewer exercise opportunities they are smaller and weaker, but "if males and females were allowed the same exercise opportunities and equal encouragement to exercise, it is thought that bodily dimorphism would diminish" (Mikkola, 2008:13). From this position, gender is not created from anything material (e.g., DNA, hormones, brain cell tissue), but entirely out of insubstantial cultural attitudes, values, and role expectations.

The Seductive Appeal of Constructionism

Perhaps the reason that radical social constructionism is so seductive is that it renders everything relative, subjective, and arbitrary. If there is nothing in the social world that is real, objective, and universal, if there are no universal standards with which to judge truth and falsity, then the search for factual knowledge of any kind is futile. If everything is relative, we are both relieved of the necessity of having to wrestle with the difficulties attending the mastery of the theories and methods of modern science with its claims of objectivity, and blessed with the freedom to deconstruct all concepts we find not to our liking. "Without scientific reasoning as the core value," assert Wright and Boisvert (2009:1232), "'theoretical imagination' is allowed to run amok." For the stubborn social constructionist with an agenda there is no need to search for empirical evidence to affirm or deny a proposition when a paragraph or two of befuddling postmodernist display prose will suffice to sweep the issue off the table and under the rug. After all, it is so much cozier to see what one believes than to believe what one sees! Thus the appeal of strong social constructionism and postmodernism is that they are more generous than science in what they will allow us to claim. As biologist and feminist Helena Cronin (2003:59–60) assesses this issue:

> It all stems from muddling science and politics. It's as if people believe that if you don't like what you think are the ideological implications of the science then you're free to reject the science—and to cobble together your own version of it instead. Now, I know that sounds ridiculous when it's spelled out explicitly. Science doesn't have ideological implications; it simply tells you how the world is—not how it ought to be. So, if a justification or a moral judgment or any such 'ought' statement pops up as a conclusion from purely scientific premises, then obviously the thing to do is to challenge the logic of the argument, not to reject the premises. But, unfortunately, this isn't often spelled out. And so, again and again, people end up rejecting the science rather than the fallacy.

An almost inevitable consequence of the embrace of strong social constructivism and the repudiation of reductionist science is the position that gender is entirely a cultural artifact (rather than partially, which we can all agree is true) that is not reducible in any way to biological sex. Thus Dorie Klein (1995:50) asserts that: "It is not the existence of the two genders that generates sexism but the other way around; in other words, women and men are not just made, but made up.... That we divide humans into two genders is a social artifact." Nowhere in Klein's work do we get any clue how we could divide humans (or any other species) into anything but the binary categories of male and female. Perhaps she means how a person with one set of genitals or the other subjectively self-identifies and behaves—how they express their masculinity or femininity. If this is what she means, then we can agree with her that this felt sense of gendered identity is culturally conditioned, but it is also biologically conditioned. Like my old wedding suit, the bimodal sex model may be a little frayed around the edges, but it is still intact and functional.

Similarly, Barrie Thorpe (1993:2; emphasis original) argues that masculinity and femininity are socially constructed via arbitrary societal norms and expectations: "Parents dress infant girls in pink and boys in blue, give them gender differentiated names and toys, and expect them to act differently.... In short, if boys and girls are different, they are not born, but *made* that way." In other words, these theorists and others like them claim that all forms of sex-differentiated socialization are entirely arbitrary historical accidents because they have no biological foundations that could direct them in any predictable ways.

Many modern feminists, having grown up with the genome project and the decade of the brain, recognize that gender is constructed around the scaffolding of sex, but softer versions of the arbitrary constructionist position still pervades feminist sociology (see Kennelly, Mertz, & Lorber, 2001). The strong constructionists' "gender from nothing" position has been called the "new secular creationism" that threatens the credibility of feminism by Barbara Ehrenreich and Janet McIntosh (1997:12). It is vital that social scientists who still hang on to the idea that nature and nurture are mutually exclusive categories let go of it and grasp something firmer. Nature needs nurture and nurture needs nature. Without nurture, nature would be a chaotic tangle of rank weeds, and without nature, nurture would have no place to go.

The Influence of Margaret Mead

If it were the case that gender differences were arbitrary social constructs decoupled from a biological substructure we should observe three different outcomes vis-à-vis gender randomly distributed across the historical and anthropological record. That is, simple probability tells us that under random (arbitrary) conditions about one-third of cultures on record would have decided to socialize the sexes in traditional ways (i.e., males to masculinity, females to femininity). One-third of the cultures would have decided to reverse this process and socialize males in feminine ways and females in masculine ways. For those who conceive of socialization as the all-powerful necessary and sufficient cause of all human attitudes, behaviors and proclivities, in such cultures females would rule the roost, beat their men, kill each other in their matriarchies at rates men do in their patriarchies, take every opportunity to bed whatever male came along, and march off to war while their men stayed home knitting socks and planting victory gardens. Finally, in about another one-third of the cultures socialization would be sex-neutral; i.e., androgynous, and neither sex would have cause to complain about the other.

Margaret Mead's *Sex and Temperament in Three Primitive Societies* (1935) became an icon for social constructionists and feminists because in it she purported to show precisely such an arbitrary socialization model. Among the Arapesh, Mundugumor, and Tchambuli (or Chambri, as they are known today) peoples of New Guinea, Mead reported the Arapesh were a gentle, cooperative people who believe that what Westerners define as a feminine temperament to be ideal for both sexes (androgenous-feminine). The violent, warlike Mundugumor people took as proper for both sexes what Westerners define as a masculine temperament (androgenous-masculine). Strangest of all were the Tchambuli who turned things on their head by favoring a feminine temperament for males and a masculine temperament for females. Mead (1935:279) reported that her "discovery" among the Tchambuli was nothing less than "a genuine reversal of the sex attitudes of our culture, with the woman the dominant, impersonal, managing partner, the man the less responsible and emotionally dependent person." Given what she purported to find among these three cultures, Mead wrote that: "We are forced to conclude that human nature is almost unbelievably malleable, responding accurately and contrastingly to cultural conditions" (1935:289).

This is cultural determinism at its worst. It views human beings as zombies programmed to act only as their cultures dictate. It is no wonder that the megalomaniacs of the world are so enamored of the blank slate view of human nature; it gives them the impression that they can pound their citizens into any shape their ideology dictates.

Mead rode this scruffy research pig into the social science theory lab where others fashioned a silk purse from its ear. The effort was immensely successful because Mead's work took on the aura of a sacred text among feminists and other social constructionists (Roscoe, 2003) and was cited widely and approvingly in introductory anthropology and sociology textbooks well into the 1990s (e.g., "Mead's research is therefore strong support for the conclusion that gender is a variable creation of society" [Macionis, 1989:317]). It is less frequently found today, however, because a number of curmudgeons demanded to actually inspect the purse, and when they did it fell apart.

Criticism of Mead's research was and is largely ignored in the anthropological, sociological, and feminist literature to which we expose our gullible students despite the fact it has been coming in since the 1930s (Brown, 1991). It turns out that sex-based temperament, behavior, and roles among the people of these cultures were not too different from what they are in other cultures around the world. Fortune's (1939) study of the Arapesh pointed out that they did not expect the two sexes to have the same temperament, that boys could only be initiated into manhood after they had committed homicide, and that warfare was a well developed art among these "gentle, feminine" people: "Violence and war were very much a part of their established tradition" (Roscoe, 2003:589). As for the Mundugumor, the males were indeed warlike and violent, but Mundugamor women expressed their "aggression" mainly by striving to please their men in ways that upstaged their co-wives, and their men folk thoroughly dominated them. Deborah Gewertz's (Gewertz, 1981; Gerwertz & Errington, 1991) fieldwork among the Tchambuli showed it to be a thoroughly male-dominant society where "aggressive" behavior on the part of women earned them a beating from their "feminine" husbands.

This is not to say that gender is not variable. Different cultures can and do mold masculine and feminine characteristics in diverse ways. As the existence of numerous Daphne Daredevils and Harvey Milquetoasts attest, there is considerable overlap between the sexes/genders on many traits, but trait variability among individuals, male or female, is attributable mainly to genetic factors (Craig, Harper, & Loat, 2004). That is, gender socialization interacts with individual temperaments to produce the ways individuals "do gender." As previously noted, genetic studies find only miniscule effects of shared environment (which includes everything siblings shared as children, including parental socialization practices) on gender roles, although they do find considerable non-shared environmental effects (McIntyre & Edwards, 2009).

However, in terms of culturally generated *average* differences, Paul Roscoe (2003), a prominent scholar of these New Guinea peoples, maintains that in relativistic terms the Arapesh *were* less warlike and aggressive than the Mundugumor and even less so than the males among the "feminine" Tchambuli. It was also true that Tchambuli males were vain and took an almost narcissistic pride in their ritualized appearance, particularly their war-paint, which Mead mistakenly took for feminine "makeup." Countless macho males around the world wear their versions of war paint (tattoos, gang colors, badges, uniforms), and preen and strut their stuff, but no one calls them "feminine" to their faces without some considerable risk.

Ecological Explanations

Many anthropologists today realize that cultural practices are underlain by the nature of their physical environment (ecology). Prominent anthropologist David Lipset (2003:699) notes (as did Mead) that the Arapesh lived in harsh mountain conditions characterized by chronic food shortages, while the Mundugumor occupied "fertile grounds, divided by small channels that were full of fish." These different ecological niches in which the Arapesh and Mundugumor lived may be sufficient to explain their different cultural "temperaments." For instance, Harpending and Draper (1988) contrasted the reproductive strategies of the !Kung bushmen, who inhabit the inhospitable Kalahari desert in South Africa, and the Mundurucu, who inhabit the resource-rich Amazon basin. Because conditions are harsh in the Kalahari, life is precarious, cooperative behavior is imperative, and "feminine" parenting effort is favored over "masculine" mating effort among the !Kung as it is among the Arapesh. The Mundurucu's rich ecology frees males for fighting, for raiding other groups, and to engage in competition for females. Mating effort is thus favored over parenting effort among the Mundurucu and the Mundugumor for ecological reasons.

Social scientists would tell us that "culture" explains the different behaviors of these peoples and leave it at that. However, such an explanation begs the question of what lies behind these cultures that makes them different. As long as social scientists view culture as an autonomous causal agent containing a more or less arbitrary grab-bag of roles, values, and customs we can never understand much about group differences in behavior. A coherent explanation of cultural differences requires an understanding of human nature and the fitness imperatives imposed on it. The peoples of all five cultures have similar evolved adaptations, but they are constrained to execute those adaptations in different environments. Only an understanding of human nature can help us to appreciate the different psychologies underlying the social behavior of people in these five cultures in ways that would lead to predictions about the behaviors of other groups inhabiting similar ecological niches (Spiro, 1999). Culture is important in explaining variation in human behavior, but it is not a realm ontologically distinct from biology.

Margaret Mead herself came to acknowledge the biasing framework supporting her "temperaments" (in her use of the term "temperament" she seemed to be wrestling with the gender concept before it existed as a social science concept). In her later work *Male and Female* (1949) she wrote: "If any human society—larger or small, simple or complex, based on the most rudimentary hunting and fishing, or on the whole elaborate interchange of manufactured products—is to survive, it must have a pattern of social life that comes to terms with the differences between the sexes" (1949:173). As with Draper and Harpending (1988), she even traced these differences to "sex differentiated reproductive strategies" (1949:160). As for her youthful claims about the Tchambuli, she later remarked: "All the claims so glibly made about societies ruled by women are nonsense. We have no reason to believe that they ever existed.... men everywhere have been in charge of running the show" (In Goldberg, 1986:31). Such statements tend to raise hackles among constructionist and liberal environmentalist feminists regardless from whose pen they come, but it marks the mature Mead as a scientist who followed the data where ever they may lead her. Predictably, I have yet to see any of these politically incorrect statements of Mead's quoted in any social science textbook discussing gender.

Melford Spiro and the Kibbutzim

Perhaps the most devastating blows to the social construction of gender argument to come from the social sciences were Melford Spiro's (1975; 1980) studies of Israel's kibbutzim. The kibbutzim movement provides us with a natural cultural experiment, the scope and size of which could never be duplicated by scientists, with which to explore the gender-as-product-of-socialization hypothesis. Begun in 1910 and heavily influenced by the Marxism of Russian immigrants, the purpose of the communal movement was to strip its members of all vestiges of "bourgeois culture" and to emancipate women from their socioeconomic and sexual shackles by abolishing sex segregation of all social roles, both public and private. Boys and girls were raised collectively, taught the same lessons, given equal responsibilities, shared the same toys, games, living quarters, and even the same toilets, dressing rooms, and showers. All this sex-neutral socialization was supposed to result in androgynous beings devoid of observable differences in nurturance, role preferences, empathy, aggression, or any other trait or behavior said to be sex-linked.

Spiro believed in the social construction of human nature and thus thought that he was setting out to discover and document the dimension of the changes in human nature brought about by the movement. What he actually found forced on him what he describes as "a kind of Copernican revolution on my own thinking" (1980:106). "As a cultural determinist," he wrote, "my aim in studying personality development in 1951 was to observe the influence of culture on human nature or, more accurately, to discover how a new culture produces a new human nature. In 1975 I found (against my own intentions) that I was observing the influence of human nature on culture" (1980:106).

What Spiro found was a counterrevolutionary feminization of the *sabra* (kibbutzim born and reared) women. Despite the decades of sex-neutral socialization and the exhortations of their ideologically committed foremothers, *sabra* women fought for formal marriage vows, for greater contact with their children, for separate toilets, showers, and living arrangements prior to marriage, for modesty of dress in the company of men, and for possession of the means of enhancing female charms. Even in an earlier work, Spiro (1975) found that the activities and fantasy lives of young children varied significantly between the sexes despite adult role models striving assiduously to eliminate those differences. As a reluctant apostate, Spiro could not fully bring himself to be explicitly biological in his interpretation on his data, preferring to write that his data supported the notion that "sexually appropriate role modeling is a function of precultural differences between the sexes" (1980:107). He was, of course, fully aware that "precultural" differences could only mean biological differences.

In common with Margaret Mead, Spiro was eventually dragged by his data to embrace biosocial explanations for gender differences, as well as a universal human nature. In his Presidential address to the Society for Psychological Anthropology (1999), Spiro detailed his intellectual journey from what he called "strong cultural determinism" and "strong cultural relativism" to a more nuanced bio-psycho-social view of human behavior. In his own words (1999:10):

> Having become increasingly disenchanted with, and bored by, the conceptual poverty of ethnographic particularism, and its mantra-like invocation of cultural determinism (now 'cultural constructionism') to explain virtually everything—and hence nothing—the work of this group [the Society for Psychological Anthropology] opened my eyes to new and exciting explanatory vistas.

Let us make no mistake, socialization is a powerful force. Without socialization we would all be barbarians; isolated creatures bereft of identity, morality, and direction, and moved only by vague feelings and emotions. Socialization can turn us into chivalrous knights or uncouth peasants, atheists or fanatical jihadists, tinkers, tailors, soldiers, sailors, beggars or thieves, but it cannot change boys into girls or girls into boys. Nothing in biosocial science counsels ignoring the power of socialization. It only counsels against granting it exclusive rights to explaining human behavior, particularly behavior that impacts the overwhelming concern of all sexually reproducing organisms—survival and reproductive success. If gender identity is constructed solely by expectations and training we would not find sexually mature individuals "socially constructed" as gays and lesbians rejecting their life-long heterosexual lessons in favor of their own privately constructed identities as homosexuals. By "privately constructed," I mean that homosexuals are conforming to the way their brains, genes, and hormones bias them despite social pressures to the contrary. These pressures have included religious and family exhortations, psychotherapy, lobotomy, aversion therapy, hysterectomy, lobotomy, imprisonment, and even the threat of death, to coerce them into heterosexuality. Heterosexual males and females are also constructing their identities in conformity with their biology as well as in conformity to their cultures, and we can no more change that than we can change a homosexual's identity. I am aware that sexual identity and gender identity are two different things. I use this example only to provide an instance showing the inability of a variety of cruel social pressures to change what is apparently innate.

Half a century ago, sociologist Dennis Wrong (1961) railed against (in his titular phrase) "The oversocialized conception of man in modern sociology." Wrong saw his discipline's view of human beings as: "sufficiently disembodied and non-materialistic to satisfy Bishop Berkeley, as well as being de-sexualized enough to please Mrs. Grundy" (1961:191). Bishop Berkeley was an 18th century philosopher who advanced a theory of immaterialism averring that things are dependent upon human perceptions for their existence, which can be seen as an early form of strong social constructionism. Mrs. Grundy was a character in an 18th century play that embodied extreme priggishness and who, for Wrong, exemplified sociologists' aversion to biology, from which they "draw back in fright" (1961:191). Criminologists, feminists or otherwise, can no longer draw back in fright if we are not to relinquish the study of crime to other less politicized and more scientifically robust disciplines. In the next two chapters I discuss evolutionary approaches to understanding gender, which provide us with an ultimate level understanding of why the genders differ so drastically in criminal behavior.

Chapter 7

Evolutionary Approaches to Gender

Human Nature

This chapter examines male and female natures and their evolutionary origins. While natural selection forges a sex-neutral human nature, sexual selection forges separate natures for males and females in all mammalian species. Humans are no exception, and thus we might say that there are two human natures—male and female (Davies & Shackleford, 2008). The features shared by the sexes (physiology, behavior, traits, characteristics, motives, and desires) dwarf the features that they do not share, or share at different average levels. But we are interested in differences rather than similarities because we are looking for answers to the gender ratio problem in criminal behavior, and the answers lie in the features that are different between the sexes; they cannot lie in features that are similar.

Criminology suffers an embarrassment of theories, all claimed by their adherents as having the "greatest amount of empirical support" (Cooper, Walsh, & Ellis, 2010:332). Cooper, Walsh, and Ellis identify ideology as contributing to our theoretical confusion and our contradictory stew of theories, but criminology's other big problem is that it lacks a meta-theory of its subject matter. We need a theory of human nature to help us separate the gold from the dross in our theories. Because human beings are as much products of evolution as all other forms of life, a growing number of leading social and behavioral scientists are "gaining enthusiasm for a Darwinian framework, which has the potential to tie together the forest of hypotheses about human behavior now out there" (de Waal, 2002:187). Evolutionary theory can provide us with that theoretical framework if we can dump the constructionist notion that humans have no nature and are so far above other animals that we cannot explain human behavior in evolutionary terms. Humans are certainly unique, but we are not uniquely unique. Every animal species is unique vis-à-vis other species, and every human being is in some way unique from every other human being given the almost infinite number of possible permutations of genes and environments that shape each person. The uniqueness of each person, however, lies in variation in the component parts of human nature, not in the central tendency of the whole. Here we are interested in what makes us the same (our shared sex-neutral human nature) and what makes us different (our sex-specific natures as males or females).

To describe the nature of anything is to list its special features and nominate those that are unique, or quantitatively enhanced, that differentiates it from everything else that is not it. For Karl Marx (1978:115) the essential being of any species is the activity that distinguishes it from every other species. For humans it is that we consciously *create* our environments instead of merely submitting to them. This free and creative activity, wrote Marx, is the distinguishing human *species being*, "man's spiritual essence, his human essence" (in Sayers, 2005:611). If this is the quintessential difference between *Homo sapiens* and the rest of the animal kingdom, the component design features that allow us to create our environments are also the human *species being*. Features such as language, intelligence, rationality, self consciousness, foresight, continuous sexual receptiveness, moral sensibility, and a myriad other features are evolutionary adaptations, and: "Human nature may be defined as our collection of adaptations" (Kennair, 2002:27).

Hunter/gatherers, agrarians, and industrial workers living in very different times and cultures will certainly express their natures differently, but these expressions are only variations on a common theme running through time and place. Melford Spiro realized this after studying vastly different cultures in Micronesia, Burma, and Israel and "came to the conclusion that I could not make sense of my findings so long as I continued to operate within the postulates of strong cultural determinism ... and ... relativism I could see no way of accounting for [my findings] short of postulating a pancultural human nature" (1999:8).

Numerous other former cultural determinists are contributing to the biosocial enterprise (see Walsh, 2009a). Like Spiro, they have been dragged (some very reluctantly) to the idea of a pancultural human nature. If there is no universal human nature underlying cultural variation, then the stories from ancient and distant cultures would be alien to us, but they are not. We understand the hopes, aspirations, character traits, personalities, emotions, feelings, goals, needs, moral strengths and weaknesses of humans in the stories of ancient and distant cultures as if they were told in the context of modern America. If culture was an arbitrary selection from a grab-bag of possibilities we would have nothing in common with humans across time and space save the necessity to satisfy our physical needs, nor could we differentiate human from non-human except by physical appearance.[1]

Natural Selection and Human Nature

All humans share a common nature by virtues of a common evolutionary history and a common genome. The human genome is the chemical archive of millions of years of evolutionary wisdom accumulated by natural selection. Any functional genes that are currently part of our genome are there because they provided some sort of advantage to our ancestors in the pursuit of the shared goals of all life-forms: survival and reproduction. Evolutionary approaches to behavior utilize the modern synthesis of natural selection and genetics to test hypotheses regarding the functional advantages conferred by these genes, or rather by the phenotypic traits that they underlie. Evolutionists are interested in distal "why" explanations rather than proximate "how" explanations. In terms of gender, for instance, endocrinologists might explain male/female differences in dominance seeking and aggression by pointing out they have different levels of testosterone (T) whereas evolutionary biologists would explore the adaptive rational for why sex differences in T exist in the first place.

Evolution is simply changes in a population's gene pool over time by the selective retention and elimination of genes as they became adaptive or maladaptive in their environments. The nature of any living thing is thus the sum of its design features that arose and promoted their increased frequency through an extended period of natural selection because they functioned to increase survival and/or reproductive success. Heritable individual differences in morphology, physiology, or behavior provide the grist of evolution.

Sociologists accept Darwinian accounts of morphological design features, but they tend not to accept that the behavioral repertoire of our species is also the result of natural selection. John Alcock (2001:223) points out the absurdity of this position: "To say that human behavior and our other attributes cannot be analyzed in evolutionary terms requires the acceptance of a genuinely bizarre position, namely, that we alone among animal species have somehow man-

---

1. The existence of a pancultural human nature is supported by a number of studies that have strongly confirmed to universality of the same personality constructs. Across at least 50 cultures with vastly different social, cultural, economic, religious, and political differences, many thousands of subjects show the same features of personality; i.e., the same recurring regularities that correlate with the same behavioral outcomes around the world (Costa, Terracciano, & McCrae, 2001; McCrae & Terracciano, 2005; Schmitt et al., 2008).

aged to achieve independence from our evolutionary history." Behavioral analysis is at the very heart of evolutionary processes. Behavior is evoked in response to environmental challenges, and natural selection passes judgment on behavior that has fitness consequences. That is, natural selection is not a "force" that induces change; it is an algorithmic process that reacts to it. Thus it is behavior that creates new variants and then, and only then, can the process of selective retention and elimination of the genes underlying them begin. Selection for behavioral traits is more rapid than for physical traits because organisms play an active part in the selection of their behavior. This is why Plomin and his colleagues assert that: "the behavioral genomic level of analysis may be the most appropriate level of understanding for evolution because the functioning of the whole organism drives evolution. That is, *behavior is often the cutting edge of natural selection*" (2003:533; emphasis added). Of course, when evolutionists speak of the evolution of behavior they are talking about behavioral *traits* and general *propensities*, not about specific behaviors.

Evolutionary accounts do not ignore culture; they simply remind us that "psychology underlies culture and society, and biological evolution underlies psychology" (Barkow, 1992:635). Ultimate level explanations complement, not compete, with proximate level explanations because nature (genes) and nurture (cultural learning) constitute a fully integrated reciprocal feedback system. Genes and culture are both information transmission devices; the former laying the foundation (the capacity) for the latter, and the latter then influencing the former (what genetic variants are useful in this culture at this time, and when and for how long should they be expressed?). If a novel trait emerges that happens to be useful and desirable in a given culture, those displaying the trait will be advantaged in terms of securing resources and mates, and thus the alleles underlying the trait will be preserved and proliferate in the population gene pool. For instance, it has been shown how genes underlying altruism can become a fixed part of the genome because it is culturally valued and thus fitness enhancing for those who demonstrate it (Gintis, 2003).

John Hawks and his colleagues (2007) have shown that the rate of genomic change has been about 100 times greater over the last 40,000 years than it was during the five-million-year long Pleistocene. They attributed this to the greater challenges posed by living in larger and larger social groups: "[T]he rapid cultural evolution during the Late Pleistocene created vastly more opportunities for further genetic changes, not fewer, as new avenues emerged for communication, social interaction, and creativity" (Hawks et al., 2007:20757). Although our most human characteristics evolved during the Pleistocene, we do not operate with brains forged exclusively during that epoch. New genetic variations affecting the brain's structure and function have been discovered as it continues to evolve in response to new ecological and cultural conditions (Evans et al., 2005; Mekel-Bobrove et al., 2005).

Sexual Selection and Gender Nature

Several Darwinian feminist scholars (Campbell, 2009; Mealey, 2000) have noted that in contrast to the images of helpless females as the pawns of powerful and oppressive males presented in sociological feminist writings, evolutionary feminist theory focuses on female choice (sexual selection) as the major mechanism that drove the evolution of sex differences. Darwinian feminists also stress that evolutionary accounts best explain why certain norms and attitudes emerged in societies, and that: "Hence, rather than a competitor to sociological theory, evolutionary theory should be considered a *necessary theoretical foundation*" (Hopcroft, 2009:1847; emphasis added). And as the mature Margaret Mead noted (see Chapter 6), it all begins with "sex differentiated reproductive strategies" (1949:160).

Charles Darwin proposed the theory of sexual selection to complete his theory of evolution, noting that while natural selection accounted for differences *between* species, it did not account for the often profound male/female differences *within* species. Natural selection avers that we should be able to explain most of the characteristics of any organism as functional adaptations; i.e., as the result of genes that have filtered across the generations because of the fitness benefits they confer. However, Darwin noted that there were many male traits that natural selection could not explain, so he completed his evolutionary theory with the notion of sexual selection. As Vandermassen (2004:11) explains: "Darwin posited sexual selection as a way to account for many conspicuous physical and behavioral traits in males. These traits are so energy demanding and so likely to make the animal vulnerable to predators, that natural selection would have normally selected them away in an early evolutionary stage." For instance, natural selection cannot explain the bright colors and elaborate morphology of peacocks' tails in terms of some survival advantage because there is none: so why is it there and why does it survive?

It survives because peahens like it. Sexual selection involves competition for reproductive partners and favors traits that lead to reproductive success, even though those characteristics may not be favored overall by natural selection. The peacock's bright plumage may attract females by indicating "good genes," but they are costly and render their possessors less likely to avoid predators. For the biologist, "fitness" is not about survival, it is a quantitative measure of reproductive success. In sexual selection terms, traits become amplified because they increased fitness by increasing the probability that their carriers were more likely than others to mate. Survival per se means nothing in evolutionary terms unless the organism passes on its genes. Sexual selection, like natural selection, causes changes in the relative frequency of alleles in populations in response to environmental challenges, but in response to sex-specific mating challenges rather than general sex-neutral challenges (Qvarnstrom, Brommer, & Gustafsson, 2006). Thus, while males and females inhabit the same ecological niches in which natural selection operates in sex neutral ways, they inhabit different mating environments that lead to sexual selection operating differently on them and consequently producing different sex-based natures.

Human female parental investment is much greater than that of males. To understand this we have to look to the principle of anisogamy, which refers to the size difference and value of the male sperm cell and the female egg cell. Sperm cells are little more than packets of chromosomes with tails that are made by the billions every day and lack nutrient value. Egg cells, on the other hand, are huge (85,000 times bigger) in comparison, are rare (one or perhaps two released each month from puberty to menopause; about 500 in total), and are rich in nutrients (Bateman & Bennett, 2006). The idea behind anisogamy is the division of labor necessary for the two gametes to unite and develop into a viable new human being. Given the rarity of egg cells, a female's unconscious imperative is to choose wisely which male she will allow to fertilize them. Males, with cheap and plentiful sperm cells can be profligate in their expenditure (Campbell, 2009).

There are two primary paths by which sexual selection proceeds: Intrasexual selection and epigamic or mate choice selection. In humans both sexes engage in both processes, but intrasexual selection is primarily male competition for access to females, and epigamic selection is a process of females choosing with whom they will mate. The more intrasexual selection operates on a species (the more competition there is for mates) the more sexual dimorphism will be selected for. In species where intrasexual selection is paramount, there are large differences between males and females in size, strength and aggression; in species where epigamic selection predominates, males are more striking in their appearance than females (Andersson & Simmons, 2006). Selection for size and strength results in males becoming much larger (up to 300% in some species) than females, and reflects a polygynous mating history in which dominance is established by physical battles among males. The fossil record shows that the earliest hominid males (*Australopithecines*) were 50 to 100 percent larger than females (Geary, 2000). The fairly low degree of sexual dimorphism for body size in *Homo sapiens* (modern men are only about 15% larger than women, on average) indicates an evolutionary shift from violent male competition for mates to a more monogamous mating system and an increase in paternal investment (Plavcan & van Schaik, 1997).

Selection for Biparental Care and Its Consequences

In humans, the evolution of biparental care and monogamous mating patterns put the skids to runaway sexual selection that breeds either enormous size (relative to female conspecifics) or costly decorations in males. Biparental care is found only in about 10% of mammalian species (Storey et al., 2006). It is found in species in which offspring remain highly dependent for a long time, where food procurement is somewhat problematic, and in which rates of predation are neither too high nor too low (Manica & Johnstone, 2004). Pair bonding will be selected for when the help of a male positively influences the probability of offspring survival by procuring food for gestating and lactating mothers and defending mother and child against predation. In precocial species with ready access to food, and with predation rates so high or so low that male parental investment is unlikely to have any positive effect on offspring survival, pair bonding is not necessary, and therefore no evolutionary pressures were exerted for its selection (Quinlan & Quinlan, 2007). Given the long period of human infant dependency, it would make sense for ancestral females to choose mates very carefully and to favor males inclined to invest resources in offspring. As Campbell (2004:17) put it: "Monogamy may have been the result of male-female coevolution of reproductive strategies, initiated by female preference for investing males." The logic of epigamic sexual selection points to the conclusion that the evolution of male traits and behavior is driven by females—human males are the way they are because our ancestral foremothers liked them that way!

What evolutionary pressures led to the selection for biparental care in humans? It was noted in Chapter 1 in the context of the origins of patriarchy that humans were on a steep evolutionary trajectory toward greater intelligence, and that greater intelligence required bigger brains. Brains are particularly voracious in their appetites for energy, thus selection for increased brain size would only result from extreme pressures, and the human brain is much larger than should be reasonably predicted for a species of our body size (Dunbar & Shultz, 2007). From the approximate 1.5 million years that separated *Australopithecus afarenis* and *Homo erectus*, hominid cranial capacity doubled from a mean of 450 cc to a mean of 900 cc, and by another 70% to about 1350 cc, from *Homo erectus* to modern *Homo sapiens* (Bromage, 1987). The increased cranial size to store increasing brain size placed tremendous reproductive burdens on females because the birth canal could not accommodate birthing infants whose brains were 60% of its adult weight as in newborn macaques, or even 45%, as in newborn chimpanzees (Hublin & Coqueugnoit, 2006). The pelvis of *Australopithecine* females was probably shaped to accommodate upright posture and bipedalism (which has the effect of narrowing the birth canal) more than to accommodate increased infant skull size, thus precipitating a conflict between the obstetric and postural requirements of ancestral females (Fieggen & Tobias, 2007). Evolutionary conflicts such as this are not uncommon; natural selection works on trajectories already in motion, and it cannot anticipate future needs.

The evolutionary mechanism that partially solved the obstetrics/posture conflict (human females have more difficulty giving birth than other species because of this problem) was for infants to be born at earlier and earlier stages of development as cerebral mass increased. Human infants experience 25% brain growth inside the womb (*uterogestation*) and 75% outside (*exterogestation*) the womb (Perry, 2002). The high degree of developmental retardation of the human brain assures a greater role for the extra-uterine environment in its development than is true of any other species.

If a species is burdened with extremely altricial young, there must have been strong selection pressures for neurohormonal mechanisms designed to assure the young would be nurtured for as long as necessary. The long period of dependency required selection for strong bonds (attachment) between mother and infant, and the extra caregiving demand on females produced selective pressure for male/female bonding. Male/female bonding probably originated with females choosing to mate with males who showed a penchant for sharing and caring rather than the more dominant and aggressive males who loved and left. Males and females who bonded to jointly provide parental investment increased the probability of their offspring surviving to reproductive age, and thus improved their reproductive success (Campbell, 2004).

Because mother/infant and male/female bonds involve an active concern for the well being of another and share crucial evolutionary goals, they share a common neurobiology (Esch & Stefano, 2005). Attachment-mediating neurohormones activate regions in the brain's reward system that are specific to either maternal or romantic love, but there are also large overlapping regions that are activated by both types of love (Bartels & Zeki, 2004). Both types of love also deactivate brain regions associated with the assessment of negative emotions and social judgments, making the lover relatively unconcerned with any negatives associated with the loved one that others may perceive. Love really is blind. Bartels and Zeki (2004:1164) conclude that this body of research brings us closer: "to understanding the neural basis of one of the most formidable instruments of evolution, which makes procreation of the species and its maintenance a deeply rewarding and pleasurable experience, and therefore ensures its survival and perpetuation."

Despite the lessening of sexual selection in our species it still operated to differentiate the sexes based on the different social roles males and females played. Recent studies of the primate brain have shown that group life has produced striking differences between the sexes in brain mechanisms related to carrying out the different demands placed on males and females in evolutionary environments (Dunbar, 2007; Lindenfors, 2005; Lindenfors, Nunn, & Barton, 2007). Because of the competitive demands of sexual selection for males, we should observe greater development of subcortical (limbic) brain structures involved in sensory-motor skills and aggression. Conversely, female fitness depends more on acquiring male resources and navigating social networks, and thus we should expect greater development of neocortical areas, particularly of the frontal lobe structures.

The studies by Patrik Lindenfors and his colleagues (2005; 2007) have shown this to be the case among 21 non-human primate species ranging from chimpanzees to rhesus monkeys. Specifically, they found that the more affiliative sociality of females is related to greater neocortex volume, and that the more competitive male sociality is more closely related to subcortical (limbic system) volume. The authors suggest that this neural sexual dimorphism should extend beyond the primate species that have been studies so far, including our own. Indeed, a functional magnetic resonance imaging (fMRI) study showed a greater ratio of orbital frontal cortex volume to amygdala volume in human females relative to males (Gur et al., 2002). The orbital frontal cortex is part of the prefrontal cortex (PFC), "the most uniquely human of all brain structures" (Goldberg, 2001:2). This vital part of the human cortex has extensive connections with other cortical regions, as well as with deeper structures in the limbic system. Because of its many connections with other brain structures it is generally considered to play the major integrative as well as a major supervisory role in the brain playing vital roles in forming moral judgments, mediating affect, and for social cognition (Romain & Reynolds, 2005). The amygdala's primary function is the storage of memories associated with the full range of emotions, particularly fear.

The Lindenfors studies also fit in well with certain aspects of genomic imprinting. Genomic imprinting is an epigenetic phenomenon that takes place in a small number of genes whereby alleles are switched off (methylated) according to their parental origin.[2] These data show that neocortical (the "social brain") volume is inherited maternally and that limbic system volume (where the amygdala is located) is inherited paternally (Dunbar, 2007; Goos & Silverman, 2001).

The Darwinian theories of natural and sexual selection are the meta-theories underlying principles of animal behavior, including the human animal, in biology. As such, it is no surprise that feminist Griet Vandermassen (2004) offers a number of reasons why the adoption of sexual selection and parental investment theories can move feminism to a higher intellectual plain. These theories, she avers, allow us to predict gender-related roles and behavior purely on a priori theoretical grounds, and that no other theory of behavior can do that. Echoing the tautology complaint made by Richard Udry in Chapter 4, she adds that: "Theories of socialization, for instance, can only predict how gender roles will affect people if one already knows what these roles are. They cannot explain why the same gender differences are reliably found all over the world" (2004:20). Vandermassen's observations should be patently obvious to everyone given that evolution is the one and only organizing principle for explaining why all animals are the way they are and do what they do.

---

2. See note 2, Chapter 5 regarding methylation.

Chapter 8

Evolutionary Explanations for Gender Differences in Criminality

Parental Investment, Staying Alive, and Fear

Anne Campbell's (1999) *staying alive* hypothesis provides an evolutionary explanation for sex differences in criminal behavior based on basic biology relevant to parental investment. It proposes that women in ancestral environments had not only less to gain from taking risks but also more to lose. Because the obligatory parental investment of females is enormously greater than that of males, and because of the infant's dependence on its mother, a mother's presence is more critical to offspring survival (and hence to the mother's reproductive success) than is a father's. Linda Mealey (2000:341) explains that throughout human evolutionary history: "Desertion of one's mother means almost certain death, whereas desertion by one's father means only a reduction in resources." There are no human cultures in which mothers desert their children anywhere near the rate of fathers (Campbell, Muncer, & Bibel, 2001). Unlike males, females are limited in the number of children they can have, so each child represents an enormous personal investment that they will not relinquish without the most compelling reasons to do so. Thus, the reproductive success of females lies primarily in parenting rather than mating effort, and this requires "staying alive."

Because a female's survival is more critical to her reproductive success (maximizing the probability that her offspring will survive) than is a male's, Campbell argues that females have evolved a propensity to avoid engaging in behaviors that pose survival risks. The practice of keeping nursing children in close proximity in ancestral environments posed an elevated risk to both mother and child if the mother placed herself in risky situations. The evolved proximate mechanism to avoid doing so is a greater propensity for females to experience more situations as fearful than do males. Fear of injury accounts for the greater ten-

73

dency of females to avoid or remove themselves from potentially violent situations, and to employ indirect and low-risk strategies in competition and dispute resolution relative to males. Her theory provides a plausible ultimate level explanation consistent with evolutionary biological principles for why the sexes differ in fear, and thus why they differ in engaging in the risky business of crime.

Fear is a basic affective state that signals danger in all animals. It is an unpleasant state of arousal most immediately experienced as a rapid increase in heart rate (tachycardia) which motivates those experiencing it to escape the immediate threat and to avoid being in similar positions in the future (Steimer, 2002). While unpleasant, it is also an adaptively functional experience that facilitates the emergence of escape/avoidance behaviors that enhances an organism's chances of survival and reproductive success.

It is invariably found that females experience fear more readily and more strongly than males whether assessed in early childhood (Kochanska & Knaack, 2003), the middle-school years (Terranova, Morris, & Boxer, 2007), or among adults across a variety of cultures (Brebner, 2003). Evidence shows that there are no sex differences in fearfulness across a number of contexts *unless* a situation contains a significant risk of physical injury. A meta-analysis of 150 risk experiment studies found that sex differences were greater when the risk involved meant actually carrying out a behavioral response than simply responding to hypothetical scenarios requiring only cognitive appraisals of possible risk (Brynes et al., 1999). Additionally, every study of gender differences in fear of crime shows that females are more fearful than males and that they assess their chances of victimization higher despite objectively being less at risk for criminal victimization (reviewed in Ellis & Walsh, 2000; Fetchenhauer & Buunk, 2005).

A part of the brain's limbic system called the amygdala is crucially involved with processing fear. Neuroimaging studies have shown sex-related hemispheric laterality of the amygdalae with males specializing to the right amygdala (specializes in detecting salient emotional stimuli) and females to the left (involved in sustained stimulus evaluation) (Cahill et al., 2004; Williams et al., 2005). As mentioned in the previous chapter, Gur and his colleagues (2002) found a highly significant greater ratio of orbital frontal cortex volume to amygdalae volume in females relative to males. Because the frontal cortices play the major cognitive role in modulating behavior, Gur and his colleagues suggested that females would be less likely to express negative emotions in aggressive ways (which could lead to injury) and to internalize stressful emotional experiences instead. A similar study found that women activate significantly more neural systems associated with emotional experiences and with encoding experience into long-term memory than men (Canli et al., 2002). The greater tendency of females to encode emotional memories means that past life events are more readily available for rumination, which increases their valence and leads to a number of anxiety and depressive disorders (assuming negative emotional memories).

Gender Differences in Status Striving

The second component of Campbell's staying alive hypothesis involves gender differences in status striving. Males exhibit greater variance in reproductive success than females but less parental certainty, and thus have more to gain and less to lose by engaging in intrasexual competition for mating opportunities (Geary, 2005; Buss, 2005; Campbell, 2009). Striving for status and dominance is a risky business in some environments. Status, respect, or "juice," is something that is hugely important for males "doing gender"; they will lie, cheat, scheme, assault, and even kill to attain it. How it is attained depends on a person's place in society and what is valued in the local culture. In environments where social controls are mostly dissolved and people are expected to take care of their own problems, a "bad ass" reputation is so highly valued that: "Many inner city young men … will risk their lives to attain it" (Anderson, 1994:89). The evolutionary reason why status is so valued by males around the world is that females are drawn to high status males because of the resources that accompany status. Because dominance and status is less reproductively consequential for females, there has been less evolutionary pressure for the selection of mechanisms useful in that endeavor for females than for males (Barash & Lipton, 2001).

Although females engage in intrasexual competition for mates, it is rarely in the form of violence and aggression in any primate species. Most of it is decidedly low key, low risk, and chronic as opposed to male competition, which is high key, high risk, and acute. A study of 20 different populations around the world found that only 2.5% of all homicides involve females killing females (Daly & Wilson, 2001), and as we have seen, when females kill they typically kill their partners in self-defense situations. The female assets most pertinent to their reproductive success are youth and beauty, which cannot be won in competition with other females; one either has them or one does not. Male assets are the resources that females desire for their reproductive success, and which can be achieved in competition with other males. Thus males are willing to incur high risks to achieve the status that bring them resources and thus access to more females, and they have evolved neurohormonal mechanisms to enable them to do so.

Campbell asserts that when females engage in crime they almost always do so for instrumental reasons, and the crimes rarely involve risk of physical injury. Both robbery and larceny/theft involve expropriating resources from others, but as seen in Figure 3.1 females constitute about 41% of arrests for larceny/theft and only about 12% of arrests for robbery (almost always with and at the instigation of male partners [Miller, 1998]), a crime carrying a relatively high risk for personal injury. There is no mention in the literature that female robbers crave the additional payoffs of dominance that male robbers do, or seek reputations as "bad asses." Aggressive females are not particularly desirable as mates, and certainly a woman with a reputation as a "bad ass" would be most unattractive. Campbell (1999:210) notes that while women do aggress and do steal, "they rarely do both at the same time because the equation of resources and status reflects a particularly masculine logic." This is essentially the same argument made by James Messerschmidt's (1993) concept of "doing gender," although Campbell's account is more scientifically sophisticated in that it is grounded in evolutionary logic indicating its ultimate origins.

Note that sex differences in aggression, dominance seeking, and promiscuity are related to parental investment, not biological sex per se. It is the level of parental investment that exerts pressure for the selection of the neural and hormonal mechanisms that underlie these sex-typical behaviors. Among certain fish and bird species in which males carry the primary burden of parental investment by incubating the eggs and feeding the young it is the female who takes the risks, has higher testosterone, and who is promiscuous and the aggressor in courtship (Barash & Lipton, 2001; Betzig, 1999). Sex-role reversal and the presence of traits that are opposite of species (mammalian) in which the females assume all or most of the burden of parenting provide support for Campbell's thesis and underlines the usefulness of cross-species comparisons.

Tending and Befriending

The "tending-and-befriending" hypothesis offered by Shelly Taylor and her colleagues (2000; 2006) augments Campbell's (1999) position. The tend-and-befriend hypothesis is a biobehavioral model of stress response, not a model of parenting, but the evolutionary pressures underlying it are clearly the result of the female parenting role. Taylor and her colleagues surveyed the rodent, primate, and human literature on coping strategies in response to stress and found a robust and consistent sex difference; females typically "tend and befriend" as opposed to the more male-typical "fight or flight" response. Tending and befriending is the tendency to respond to environmental stressors by drawing closer to offspring and intensifying their care and by drawing closer to social support networks of other females. Of course, males tend and be-friend in response to threat, but they do not do so in the same ways, to the same degree, or in response to the same stresses and threats as females, and fe-males do fight or flee when conditions demand it, but they do so in different ways and to different degrees. The tendency among females apparently arose to protect themselves and their children in situations in which the male response of fighting or fleeing were not viable options. When there are no other options, then females will flee with their young and fight fiercely to protect them.

The female inclination to tend and befriend is assumed to have coevolved from the more primitive attachment and nurturing systems chemically organized and sustained by oxytocin (OT). OT is a phylogenically ancient peptide synthesized in certain nuclei of the hypothalamus; it is vitally important to mammalian attachment, and is often referred to as "the cuddle chemical" because it "calms and connects" (MacDonald & MacDonald, 2010). Among other things, OT facilitates uterine contractions, parturition, lactation, and partner bonding, but its psychological function is to motivate the desire for offspring contact, which is obviously a huge benefit for offspring. As Campbell (2008:2) asserts, although OT operates in both males and females, it is especially relevant for females because "OT and OT receptors are regulated by estrogen. Estrogen receptor ß is expressed in hypothalamic neurons that synthesize OT, and estrogen receptor α is needed for the synthesis of OT receptors in the amygdala." Brain pleasure centers such as the nucleus accumbens is a major target for OT (MacDonald & MacDonald, 2010), which demonstrates that natural selection builds reward systems for behaving in ways that lead to survival and reproductive success.

Most stress encountered by males in evolutionary environments came from either other males in the competition for status and access to females or from predators in the hunting/hunted nature of primitive food acquisition. The first case implies "fight or forfeit mating" and the second implies "take risks or starve." Whether an organism fights or flees depends on if it perceives the threat as surmountable. These male typical responses are driven by testosterone (T), which works antagonistically to OT (Taylor, 2006). When men befriend in the face of threat, T tends to rise in anticipation of aggressive responses (Geary & Flinn, 2002).

In most threat situations faced by females in evolutionary environments, the fight or flight response would not be viable. If threat came from an aggressive male, a woman was unlikely to outfight or outrun him. If the threat came from a non-human predator, fleeing would mean abandoning her offspring to their fate. A more adaptive response in both cases was to hunker down and tend to her offspring and to turn to her social network of other females to help with her defense. The initial physiological stress response is identical in males and females; i.e., arousal of the autonomic nervous system (ANS), but the response is down-regulated in females by oxytocin, which reduces amygdala activity and increases parasympathetic ANS activity (MacDonald & MacDonald, 2010).

The ANS has two branches: the sympathetic and the parasympathetic. When an organism perceives a threat to its well-being the sympathetic system immediately mobilizes the body for vigorous action by pumping out the hormone epinephrine (adrenaline). The parasympathetic system (the "rest and digest" system) restores the body to homeostasis (the return of physiological functions to their "set-points" of acceptable range values) after the organism perceives the threat is over. As the tend-and-befriend hypothesis would lead us to suspect, a large number of studies have shown that there are fundamental sex differences in the organization of ANS functioning (reviewed in Sax, 2006). In males, the sympathetic branch dominates with the primary neurotransmitter being norepinephrine (noradrenaline) and the primary hormone being epinephrine (adrenaline). In females, the parasympathetic branch is dominant, with acetylcholine being both the primary neurotransmitter and humoral factor. According to Sax (2006:192), the activation of the ANS in females *tends* to result in slowing or freezing and is experienced as unpleasant and stressful. In males, on the other hand, it *typically* results in sharpened senses and is often subjectively experienced as thrilling.

The tend-and-befriend hypothesis is useful to us in understanding the ultimate evolutionary and proximate hormonal mechanisms that underlie the tendency for women to be less physically aggressive when threatened. Studies indicate no sex differences in the frequency or intensity of anger or an insignificant tendency for women to experience anger more frequently. However, men are more likely to express anger via confrontation and verbal and/or physical aggression against those who have threatened and angered them. The female tendency is to discuss the situation (venting) with a friend or other uninvolved individual or to cry and seek solace (Campbell, 2006).

Specific Evolutionary Theories of Criminal Behavior

The evolutionary theories of criminal behavior relevant to gender differences are *cheater theory*, *conditional adaptation theory*, and *alternative adaptation theory.* The foundation for all three theories is reproductive strategies (mating effort versus parenting effort) and the tactics that flow from them. Mating effort is the proportion of one's reproductive effort invested in finding sexual partners, and parenting effort is the proportion invested in caring for offspring.

Research shows that a heavy emphasis on mating effort is strongly linked to criminality. A review of 51 studies found that 50 of them reported a significant positive relationship between the number of sex partners and criminality, and another review of 31 studies found that age of onset of sexual behavior was significantly inversely related to criminal behavior in all 31 (Ellis & Walsh, 2000). A British cohort study found that the most antisocial 10 percent of males in the cohort fathered 27 percent of the children (Jaffee et al., 2003). At the molecular genetic level, Guo and his colleagues (2007) found that males who were homozygous for the 10-repeat dopamine transporter (DAT1) gene had 80 to 100 percent (depending on age category) more sex partners than males who were homozygous for the 9-repeat version. These findings did not apply to females, however, which underlies the non-deterministic nature of genes. Another study found the same DAT1 polymorphism that was significantly related to number of sex partners was also significantly related to antisocial behavior among a large sample of males between the ages of 18 and 26 (Beaver, Wright, & Walsh, 2008).[1]

Cheater Theory

Cheater theory rests on the broad asymmetry between the reproductive strategies of males and females, with male reproductive success more variable. This is particularly so in polygynous, and possibly so in human evolutionary environments. Females have a much lower potential reproductive ceiling than males, although almost all females will probably reproduce. The major factor in female reproductive success has been to secure and hold on to the assistance of a mate to raise her offspring. Given lower variation but greater reproductive certainty, females have evolved a mating strategy inclining them to be choosier about whom they will mate with than males are (Badcock, 2000; Cartwright; 2000).

---

1. Polymorphisms are the genetic variations that make us all different from one another. The two major polymorphisms being single nucleotide polymorphisms (SNPs) and micro- and mini-satellites (referred to collectively as variable number of tandem repeats—VNTRs). A difference in just one nucleotide is all that differentiates one allele from another in a SNP. VTNRs differ from one another in the length of contiguous nucleotide bases that are repeated a different number of times. The more times the sequence of nucleotides is repeated, the longer the allele (the gene alternate carrying the polymorphism).

Because male reproductive success is potentially greater the more females they can gain sexual access to, evolutionary logic concludes that males should have a strong evolved desire for multiple partners. Males can respond to the more reticent female strategy in one of two ways: They can either trick or force a female to have sex and then move on to the next female or they can comply with female preferences and assist a single female in raising their offspring. The first strategy has been called the *Cad* strategy, and the second the *Dad* strategy (Cashdan, 1993). Almost all heterosexual males have probably used cheater tactics (falsely proclaiming love and fidelity and the use of some form of coercion) to obtain sex in their youth, but the vast majority will eventually settle down and assist a female to raise their young. The *Dad* strategy is facilitated by the social emotions, particularly love (Aron et al., 2005). The *Cad* strategy is likely to be followed across the life course by males who are deficient in the social emotions.

Cheater theory does not postulate that the Cad strategy reflects a defective genome, but rather that it reflects a normal, albeit morally regrettable, alternative adaptive strategy. The posited mechanism aiding cads (and criminals) is the down regulation of the social emotions so that they are unlikely to experience guilt, shame, anxiety, and empathy. Because chronic cheats operate "below the emotional poverty line" (Hare, 1993:134), they do not reveal clues that would allow others to judge their intentions. Lacking an emotional basis for self-regulation, chronic cheats make social decisions exclusively on the basis of rational cost/benefit calculations (Viding et al., 2005, Weibe, 2009). The quintessential cheat/cad/criminal is, of course, the psychopath, and numerous brain imaging studies have revealed the inability of the psychopath to tie together the rational and emotional hemispheres of the brain (reviewed in Walsh & Wu, 2008). David Rowe (2002a:62–63) provides a thumbnail sketch of the traits useful in supporting the Cad mating strategy, which are the same traits useful in pursuing criminal activities.

> A strong sexual drive and attraction to novelty of new sexual partners is clearly one component of mating effort. An ability to appear charming and superficially interested in women while courting them would be useful. The emotional attachment, however, must be an insincere one, to prevent emotional bonding to a girlfriend or spouse. The cad may be aggressive, to coerce sex from partly willing partners and to deter rival men. He feels little remorse about lying or cheating. Impulsivity could be advantageous in a cad because mating decisions must be made quickly and without prolonged deliberation; the unconscious aim is many partners, not a high-quality partner.

Conditional Adaptation Theory (CAT)

CAT proposes that people adopt different reproductive strategies based on early childhood experiences (Belsky & Draper, 1991). CAT includes features that allow for predictions about the involvement of women as well as men in antisocial behavior, and includes the *whore* vs. *Madonna* dichotomy in addition to the *cad* vs. *dad* dichotomy. Both male and female criminals and serious delinquents have significantly more sex partners and begin sexual activity earlier than do persons in general. CAT proposes that females will tend to achieve early menarche and adopt an unrestricted (promiscuous) sexual strategy if they learned during their childhood that interpersonal relationships are ephemeral and unreliable (as indexed by such things as parental divorce and witnessing others engaging in short-term relationships). Females who learned the opposite will tend to adopt a more restricted strategy. Neither strategy is consciously chosen, of course, but rather flows from subconscious expectations based on early experiences of the stability/instability of interpersonal relationships.

The traits underlying the cad/whore/mating and dad/Madonna/parenting strategies are highly heritable, so individuals may vary in their susceptibility to adopt a particular reproductive strategy for genetic reasons rather than early childhood experiences. In other words, the negative and ephemeral relationships observed among the sexually unrestricted may be a *consequence* of their strategy rather than a cause. Children receive a suite of genes as well as an environment from their parents, and the similarity of parent/offspring sexual strategies may have more to do with shared genes than shared environments (Walsh, 2000). Empirical support for this interpretation is supplied by Rowe (2002b), who found heritability coefficients of 0.50, 0.54, and 0.28 for age at menarche, non-virgin status, and age at first intercourse, respectively.

Alternative Adaptation Theory (AAT)

AAT proposes that humans are arrayed along a continuum regarding where they have a tendency to focus their reproductive efforts (mating vs. parenting) largely for genetic reasons. The best demographic predictors of where reproductive effort is focused are gender and age, which are also the best demographic predictors of crime and delinquency (Walsh & Beaver, 2009). Males and the young emphasize mating effort and females and older persons emphasize parenting effort. The suite of traits useful for focusing on mating effort, such as impulsiveness and aggression are also useful in pursuing criminal activity, and traits useful for parenting effort, such as empathy, conscientiousness, and altruism, are also useful for prosocial, activity: "crime can be identified with the behaviors that tend to promote mating effort and noncrime with those that tend to promote parenting effort" (Rowe, 1996:270).

AAT makes the same predictions CAT does regarding early onset of sexual behavior and number of sexual partners, but explains the relationship by indicating that both criminal activity and a high level of mating effort is sustained by the same suite of heritable traits. AAT places little emphasis on childrearing because behavior genetic studies consistently show that common rearing environment (which is stressed by CAT) has little or no lasting influence on offspring personality or cognitive traits.

In sum, all evolutionary theories of gender differences in criminal behavior (as well as intrasexual differences) aver that a reproductive strategy emphasizing mating effort is similar to criminal behavior in that direct and immediate methods are used to procure resources illegitimately without much thought being given to the consequences either to the self or to the victim. Conversely, parenting effort is embedded in a prosocial lifestyle in which resource procurement relies on the patient and intelligent accumulation of social and occupational skills that are attractive to females. Thus, reproductive strategies mirror antisocial/prosocial behavior in terms of emphases on immediate versus delayed gratification.

Chapter 9

From Genes to Gender: Sexual Differentiation of the Brain

The Neurohormonal Basis of Gender

The human brain is the immensely complicated magnum opus of millions of years of evolution. This biological wonder comprises only about two percent of body mass but takes 60% of its genes to construct, and consumes 25% of the body's glucose energy and 20% of its oxygen as it perceives, evaluates, and responds to its environment (Jung et al., 2009). All stimuli both internal and external are necessarily mediated by the brain because the brain is where genetic dispositions and environmental experiences are integrated. Because of this the basics of neuroscience must be part of every criminologist's toolkit, particularly those trying to understand the proximate foundations (as opposed to the ultimate evolutionary foundations) of the gender ratio problem. Powerful brain imaging technologies allowing for in vivo assessment of brain structure and function have resulted in an explosion of new information on the neural correlates of traits and characteristics related to criminal behavior, including gender (or perhaps more correctly, sex) over the past two decades. Although we are a long way from fully understanding the brain, we ignore what is known at our peril. As Matt Robinson (2004:72) reminds us, any theory of behavior "is logically incomplete if it does not discuss the role of the brain."

Biosocial explanations of gender differences rest on a foundation of differential neurological organization shaped by a complicated mélange of prenatal genetic and hormonal processes which in turn reflect evolutionary pressures that weighed differently on the sexes. Meta-analyses have shown that most measured gender differences are small and relatively inconsequential, but the differences that are most salient to core gender identity; i.e., at the center of one's identity as male or female, are very large (reviewed in

Hines, 2004). Not surprisingly, these core gender differences are precisely the traits that are most strongly and positively related to criminal behavior (aggression, callousness, impulsiveness, etc.) or negatively related (empathy, altruism, nurturance), all of which are undergirded by differential neurobiology (in terms of mean sex differences) and genetic polymorphisms (in terms of within-sex variation).

Feminist neuroscientist Doreen Kimura informs us that sex-specific evolutionary pressures assure that males and females arrive in this world with "differently wired brains," and these brain differences "make it almost impossible to evaluate the effects of experience [the socialization process] independent of physiological predisposition" (1992:119). Sarah Bennett and her colleagues (2005:273) concur, and explain the pathways from sex-differentiated brain organization to antisocial behavior:

> Males and females vary on a number of perceptual and cognitive information-processing domains that are difficult to ascribe to sex-role socialization.... the human brain is either masculinized or feminized structurally and chemically before birth. Genetics and the biological environment in utero provide the foundation of gender differences in early brain morphology, physiology, chemistry, and nervous system development. It would be surprising if these differences did not contribute to gender differences in cognitive abilities, temperament, and ultimately, normal or antisocial behavior.

Thus male vulnerability to antisocial behavior is largely a function of their exposure to neurochemicals in utero. The major hormonal factor differentiating maleness from femaleness and which underlies gender differences in aggression, violence, and antisocial behavior in general, is testosterone (T) (Kanazawa, 2003). No reputable scientist claims that T is a major independent and direct cause of criminal behavior, only that it facilitates such behavior and that it is the major factor that ultimately underlies gender *differences* in criminal behavior. Both sexes produce T, but males have basal levels of T about 10 times higher (Ellis, 2005). What differentiates the sexes more than basal T levels is the level of free T, since only free T is biologically active. Most circulating T is bound to sex hormone binding globulin (SHBG), which renders it inactive. Bound testosterone cannot interact with androgen receptors on cells, and females have an average of twice as much SHBG, which means that males have about 20 times as much active T as females (Hryb et al., 2002).

Sexing the Brain

Neuroscientist Jeanette Norden (2007:117) states that: "Male and female brains can be distinguished on the basis of how particular structures are organized at gross, cellular, or even molecular levels." De Vries and Sodersten (2009:589) concur: "Thousands of studies have documented sex differences in the brain in practically any parameter imaginable." These brain sex differences begin with the sex chromosomes that specify either an XX female or an XY male and are encoded in the genes present on the sex chromosomes: "These genes are differentially represented in the cells of males and females, and have been selected for sex-specific roles. The brain is a sexually dimorphic organ and is also shaped by sex-specific [evolutionary] selection pressures" (Arnold, 2004:1).

Sex differentiation begins with the Y chromosome, a puny little creature that probably evolved (as did the X) from a pair of autosomes in ancestral vertebrates many millions of years ago (Xu & Disteche, 2006). The male-specific Y chromosome has only 27 genes coding for proteins on it whereas the X (shared by both males and females) encodes for about 1,500 (Arnold et al., 2009). Moreover, many Y genes have homologous genes on the X chromosome, which reduces the functional differences in XY and XX cells (Arnold et al., 2009). This leaves precious few genes that are male specific, and perhaps only one that really is, and that is the SRY ("sex-determining region of the Y chromosome") gene. If anyone was foolish enough to claim that there is in any sense a "crime gene," the SRY in the only candidate.

In all mammalian species, maleness is induced from an intrinsically female form by processes initiated by the SRY gene. All XY individuals would develop as females without the SRY gene, and XX individuals have all the material needed to make a male except this one gene. The SRY gene is a necessary but not sufficient step toward masculinization, and it is not all-powerful. There are rare cases when a double dose of a gene called DAX-1 on a male's X chromosome, which normally is part of forming the testes, suppresses SRY-stimulated testes development. In such cases the XY karyotype, SRY gene and all, develop as a female (Allen, 2007).

The major function of the SRY gene, and its downstream genetic cohorts, such as the autosomal SOX9 gene and the sex chromosomal DAX-1 gene, is to induce the development of the testes from the undifferentiated gonads rather than the ovaries that would otherwise develop in its absence. The testes then produce androgens, the major one being T, which when transformed by the enzyme aromatase into estradiol (curiously, since this is the hormone that induces feminization at puberty) will masculinize the brain by saturating neurons with the appropriate T receptors, and as a result "the structure and functioning of these regions become altered, as are the behaviors they control ... high concentrations of prenatal androgens result in male-typical behavior ... female-typical behavior develops in the absence of androgens" (Yang, Baskin, & DiSandro, 2010:154). The testes also produce Mullerian inhibiting substance (MIS), regulated by the SOX9 gene, which causes the atrophy of internal female sex organs (Swaab, 2004).

Brain masculinization is not an all-or-nothing process. Rather, it is one that describes a continuum that may contain significant XX/XY overlap. Thus sex/gender lies on a continuum from extreme femaleness (which we can define as the complete absence of androgens or insensitivity to them) to extreme maleness (which we can define as significantly above average levels of androgens). The female fetus is protected from the diverting effects of androgen, but not completely. Once prenatal androgens have sensitized receptors in the male brain to their effects, there is a second surge from about the second week of life to about the sixth month of life that further "imprints" the male brain, and then the third surge at puberty that activates the brain to engage in male-typical behavior (Sisk & Zehr, 2005). All the additional steps required to switch the male brain from its "default" female form is the reason that significantly more males than females suffer from all kinds of neurological problems (ADHD, dyslexia, autism, Asperger's syndrome, stuttering, language delays, and so forth) because things can go awry when perfectly good systems are meddled with.[1]

Intersex Anomalies: What Can They Tell Us about Gender Differences?

Gender socialization is so strongly confounded by biological sex (i.e., female sex becomes overwhelmingly gendered feminine and male sex over-

---

1. It should be noted that this is an extremely simplified account of human sexual differentiation. The SRY gene is a regulator or "switch" gene that turns on a number of other genes. It is only activated prenatally for a short time at various intervals, itself being regulated by autosomal genes that it regulates in a reciprocal feedback way. It is the downstream autosomal genes that go about the business of actually constructing the testes. Fourteen different genes, including two on the X chromosome (no others on the Y) have been identified as contributing to mammalian sex determination. A mutation of one of them on chromosome 11, known as the WT1 gene, leads to yet another intersex condition known as Denys-Drash Syndrome (DDS). DDS results in an XY karyotype with ambiguous or completely feminized genitalia, although behavior is male biased. There are even cases of XX karyotypes that develop male phenotypes due to the SRY gene crossing over from the Y to the X during spermatogenesis (Rosario, 2009).

whelmingly becomes gendered masculine) that it is difficult to untangle the relative contributions of biology and socialization to gender-typical behavior. Kenneth Zucker (2002:6) points out that this difficulty has led a number of researchers "to the study of children with intersex conditions in the hope of providing at least a partial solution to the problem." Intersex individuals (pseudo-hermaphrodites) are "experiments of nature" born with a number of congenital conditions in which chromosomal/gonadal sex does not necessarily comport with anatomical sex. Using the anomalous to gain insight into the "normal" is a well-worn backdoor approach in science. Species mutants serve biologists to clarify the species norm, and brain-damaged patients provide neuroscientists with a wealth of information about the organization of the normal cognitive system. Likewise, the study of human intersex individuals can provide behavioral scientists with important clues as to the extent to which gendered behavior rests on biological sex by examining the behavioral effects of prenatal hormones (or their absence) on these individuals (Gooran, 2006).

Androgen-insensitivity syndrome (AIS): AIS is a syndrome in which the receptor sites of XY males that normally bind androgens are partially (PAIS) or completely (CAIS) inoperative due to a mutation of the androgen receptor gene located on the X chromosome. If the receptors are completely inoperative, the male XY genotype develops a completely female phenotype. Because CAIS individuals have the SRY gene they have androgen-producing testes (undescended) but, because their androgen receptors are insensitive to its effects, the internal male sex structures do not develop. Since the testes secrete normal amounts of MIS, CAIS individuals have neither male nor female internal sex organs, although the external genitalia are unambiguously female (although the vagina is shallow and leads to a dead end). This condition is not diagnosed until AIS individuals consult a physician about failure to menstruate or about painful intercourse. Unresponsive to the masculinizing effects of androgens on the brain, CAIS individuals tend to be extremely beautiful and feminine in appearance. They conform to typical attitudinal, trait, and behavioral patterns of normal females, often exaggeratedly so, and remain comfortable with their sexual and gender identities after their condition is revealed to them (Jurgensen et al., 2007).

PAIS individuals tend to be behaviorally intermediate in terms of gendered behavior. PAIS occurs less frequently than CAIS and because they are only partially insensitive to androgens the completeness of their genitalia varies with the degree of androgen resistance. PAIS children are assigned and reared as males or females primarily according to the degree of genital virilization because the degree of genital virilization indexes the degree of brain masculinization. Most PAIS individuals report satisfaction with their sex/gender identity (Byne, 2006).

Congenital adrenal hyperplasia (CAH): Classic CAH is caused by a deficiency in 21-hydroxlase, an enzyme that helps to convert progesterone to cortisol. The deficiency leads to a buildup in progesterone (a precursor of T), resulting in high levels of interuterine T and low levels of cortisol (Meyer-Bahlburg et al., 2006). These excess androgens result in extremely precocious sexual development in males and variable degrees of masculinization of the genitalia and brains of females. The degree of masculinization of the genitalia (a penis-like clitoris and some degree of fusion of the labia) indexes the degree to which the brain has been masculinized. However, because even the most virilized of girls have internal female organs capable of reproduction, most authorities recommend female assignment via hormonal treatment and surgery despite the high risk involved of such girls later rejecting that assignment (Byne, 2006).

CAH females engage in significantly more male-typical behavior and possess more male-typical traits than non-CAH females, such as a liking for rough and tumble play, better visual-spatial than verbal skills, lower maternal interests, less interest in marriage, a greater interest in careers, and a greater probability of bisexuality and homosexuality (about one-third of them so describe themselves [Gooren, 2006]). They score higher on more male-typical skill (e.g., visual-spatial skills) than their unaffected sisters and tend to dislike feminine frills such as jewelry and makeup and playing with dolls, again suggesting that toy preferences are not arbitrary (Garrett, 2009). Although there are no studies directly assessing criminal behavior among CAH women, because they score higher than hormonally normal women on traits positively associated with crime, and lower on traits negatively associated with crime (maternal interest, commitments to relationships), they are likely to be present in female criminal populations in numbers relatively greater than their numbers in the general population.

There are also less dramatic but significant behavioral consequences caused by prenatal exposure to androgens among females who are not considered intersex. Female fetuses exposed to androgenizing drugs such as diethylstilbestrol (DES) show masculine behavioral patterns as girls and women (Garrett, 2009) and are at a markedly higher risk of homo- or bi-sexuality than non-exposed females (Gooren, 2006). DES, taken to prevent miscarriages, was taken off the market after its effects became apparent. There are also some masculinizing effects noted for females who shared a womb with a male co-twin (Craig, Harper, & Loat, 2004), and a longitudinal cohort study by Hines and her colleagues (2002) reported a positive linear relationship between fetal T collected from amniotic fluid and degree of masculinized gender behavior in young girls measured by toy, playmate, and activity preferences. The extent to which prenatally androgen-exposed females move toward typical male preferences most likely depends on the extent of that exposure (Hines, 2006).

The XYY syndrome: The XYY syndrome is the anomaly that has generated more interest than any other in criminology, and has a rate of approximately 1 per 1,000 male births (Briken et al., 2006). The XYY male is not a "supermale" or a "born criminal" as used to be thought, but he is significantly more likely than XY males to evidence exaggeration of male-typical behavioral traits. Most descriptions of the behavioral phenotype suggest that in comparison with normal XY males, XYY males have higher levels of aggression, hyperactivity, impulsiveness, an unbalanced intellectual profile (a performance IQ significantly greater than verbal IQ), and atypical brain-wave patterns (Briken et al., 2006; O'Brien, 2006). Plasma testosterone concentrations of XYY men are usually found to be significantly higher than in matched samples of normal XY men. Although most XYY males lead fairly normal lives, they are at elevated risk for a diagnosis of psychopathy and for committing sex crimes, and they are imprisoned or in psychiatric hospitals at rates greatly exceeding their incidence in the general population (Briken et al., 2006).

Another interesting intersex condition is an enzymatic condition known as *5-alpha-reductase deficiency* (5-ARD). Because of this deficiency, T cannot be converted to dihydrotestosterone (DHT), which is the androgen required for normal in utero masculinization of the external genitalia. Thus, 5-ARD males are born with ambiguous or completely female genitalia and are almost always reared as girls. However, at puberty T rather than DHT is responsible for the emergence of male secondary sexual characteristics and the growth of the genitalia, thus in 5-ARD males the testes descend and the "clitoris" markedly enlarges to become a penis, which varies considerably in the degree of virilization (size). In one study of 18 5-ARD boys who had been reared as girls from birth, 17 changed to a male gender identity at puberty (Diamond, 1999). There are a number of other studies of 5-ARD individuals that report around a 90% gender switch at puberty (see Byne, 2006), although a study of 25 Brazilian female-raised 5-ARD males only 13 (52%) changed to male identity at puberty (Mendonca et al., 2003). The varying proportions of gender changing may reflect different cultural attitudes regarding gender.

On the other hand, individuals with a condition called *17beta-hydroxysteroid dehydrogenase deficiency* (17-BHSD) show less dramatic gender changes at puberty. These individuals are also XY males born with ambiguous or fully female genitalia and are typically reared as girls. At puberty these boys develop similarly to 5-ARD boys, but only about 50% switch gender identity (Gooren, 2006). The different rate of gender switching between 5-ARD and 17-BHSD individuals is probably a function of the roles of the two different enzymes involved. In 5-ARD individuals the problem is conversion of T to DHT, which does not affect T's role in masculinizing the brain. In 17-BHSD individuals, the deficiency is in the enzyme that catalyzes the final step in T synthesis, thus leading to a deficit of T available for brain masculinization in utero (Byne, 2006).

Other "Intersex" Conditions

Perhaps even more interesting than intersex anomalies in terms of the effects of prenatal hormones on behavior are chromosomally male infants who lack a penis for one reason or another. These conditions are ablatio penis (traumatic loss of penis), cloacal exstrophy (a severe birth defect wherein the bladder and intestines are turned inside out and exposed and the penis split, absent, or severely deformed), and penile agenesis (born without a penis). Males with these conditions have brains that have presumably been masculinized, but because of their abnormal penis status they are typically surgically assigned as females and reared as such.

Ablatio penis is best illustrated by the well-publicized case of David Reimer (popularly known as the John/Joan case) who had his penis mutilated in a botched circumcision. In conformity with the extreme environmental ideas about gender in the 1970s, surgeons castrated David and fashioned a vagina for him. He was given estrogen injections and reassigned as a female with the name Brenda. John Money, the major proponent of gender neutrality at birth in the 1970s, assured Brenda's parents that Brenda would become a well-adjusted woman. All surgical, hormonal, and socialization efforts to turn David into Brenda failed dramatically in every respect. When he learned of his medical history he expressed relief and underwent further surgery to construct a penis (nonfunctioning). The whole tragic story (David committed suicide in 2004) is told in Colapinto (2006). Because of this and five other similar cases of assigned gender rejection cataloged by Diamond (1999), Money came to reject the notion of gender neutrality at birth: "Clearly, the brain holds the secrets of the etiology of gender identity differentiation" (Money, 1986:235).

Conversely, Bradley, Oliver, Chernick, and Zucker (1998) report on another infant male reassigned as a female due to loss of his penis during circumcision and raised as a female who was still living as a woman at age 28. This individual reported comfort with the assigned gender but always worked at "male" occupations, had male-typical interests, considered herself bisexual, reported that her sexual fantasies were all of females, and was living in a "lesbian" relationship at the time of interview. Thus self-defined gender can be inconsistent with gendered behavior and sexual orientation.

A review of 50 cloacal exstrophy patients found that over half of the XY female-raised patients displayed male behavior patterns and questioned their gender identity, and all displayed interests and attitudes typical of males despite early castration to avoid the neonatal T surge (Woo, Thomas, & Brock, 2009). According to one review, about half of male individuals with penile ablation, penile agenesis, or cloacal exstrophy maintain their assigned gender identities, although this is usually assessed in childhood before the third activation surge of T at puberty; there is an increased probability of rejecting the assigned identity as individuals age (Meyer-Bahlburg, 2005). Byne (2006) reports on one XY exstrophy patient raised as a female who underwent a complete sex/gender change at age 52 only after both his parents had died.

The fact that most female-reared XY males change to a male identity in spite of incongruent genitalia, exogenous estrogens administered to facilitate female physical appearance, and gender socialization, the change represents the triumph of a virilized brain in what must be a series of stupendous psychologically distressing battles. It is not really that surprising that some would choose to retain their assigned gender in the face of internal and external pressures to do so. After all, these individuals are presented with a fait accompli in that they have visibly female sex organs, they have been treated all their lives as females, and they realize that there is presently no way that surgeons can fashion a functioning penis for them. One the other hand, those few who maintain their gender of rearing offer some evidence that gender identity is not completely or overwhelmingly determined by biology.

Although the facilitative influence of T does not appear strong enough to account for much variance in aggression and various forms of antisocial behavior when assayed solely within the normal male range, the normal male range is a restricted one in a larger distribution across the full range of human possibilities. Intersex anomalies reflect extreme variance in androgen levels ranging from complete insensitivity to it (CAIS), to the upper level of the normal male range (XYY males). The rarity of these anomalies renders the evidence sparse, but it is both consistent and convincing: male-typical behaviors, including antisocial behaviors of all kinds, increase as we move from extreme femininity to extreme masculinity as defined by androgen levels.[2] While some

---

2. According to Fausto-Sterling (2002), about 1.7% of individuals are born with some sort of intersex problem. If the true percentage is, say, only 1%, then that translates into approximately 3 million individuals in the United States born with one of these intersex conditions.

may continue to insist that the male/female gap in antisocial behavior is explicable in terms of socialization, it would require extraordinary sophistry to similarly explain the pattern revealed here. Social science has no theory capable of making sense of this pattern, but an understanding of the behavioral organizing effects of gonadal steroids circulating in the developing fetal brain renders it fully intelligible (Walsh, 1995).

In light of all the prenatal processes bombarding the zygote/embryo/fetus, one cannot help but be impressed by the amazing prescience of 19th century British romantic poet and novelist, Samuel Taylor Coleridge. Long before anyone had heard of genes, chromosomes, or hormones, Coleridge wrote: "The history of man for the nine months preceding his birth would, probably, be far more interesting and contain events of greater moment than for all the three score and ten years that follow it" (cited in Hepper, 2005:474). It is this intrauterine environment that places us on a gender trajectory that socialization cannot derail—nature plants gender and nurture cultivates it, but nurture does not and cannot plant it.

Chapter 10

Sex/Gender Differences in Brain Structure and Function

Basic Brain Development

Nothing I have said about the brain in previous chapters or will say in this one gainsays the power of learning, including learning to "do" gender. Learning takes place in the brain, and the brain itself depends on learning for its own development. Although as noted in the previous chapter that about 60% of the human genome is involved in brain development (Mitchell, 2007), there are too few genes relative to the billions of neurons and the trillions of connections they can make with one another to completely specify that development. Our experiences, not our genes, will largely specify the connection patterns of our neurons. If genes alone had been assigned the task of specifying neuronal connections, we would all be hard-wired drones incapable of adapting to novel situations; human environments are much too varied and much too complex for hard-wired brains.

Neuroscientists identify two brain developmental processes that *physically* capture environmental events: *experience-expected* and *experience-dependent* (Edelman, 1992; Schon & Silven, 2007). Experience-expected mechanisms are hard-wired and reflect the brain's phylogenic history; experience-dependent mechanisms reflect the brain's ontogenic plasticity. These two processes tell us that while every member of a species inherits identical hard-wired brain structures and functions produced by a common pool of genetic material, individuals will vary in brain functioning as their genes interact with their environments to softwire their brains (Depue & Collins, 1999; Gunnar & Quevedo, 2007). The distinction between the two processes is illustrated by language, the *capacity* for which is an entirely hard-wired experience-expected capacity, but what language(s) a person speaks is entirely the result of softwired experience-dependent processes.

Certain abilities and processes such as sight, speech, depth perception, affectionate bonds, mobility, and sexual maturation are vital, and natural selection has provided for mechanisms (adaptations) designed to take advantage of experiences occurring naturally within the normal range of human environments. These are the hardwired experience-expected processes that have evolved as a readiness of the brain at certain "critical" developmental periods to assimilate environmental information into its neural pathways that is vital to an organism and ubiquitous in its environment. Some things are so important that they cannot be left to the vicissitudes of learning. Pre-experiential brain organization frames and orients our experiences so that we will respond consistently and stereotypically to vital stimuli (Geary, 2005). It is not surprising, then, that many of the sex-related traits associated with the roles played by our distant ancestors have insinuated themselves into our neural architecture as experience-expected mechanisms.

Experience-dependent brain development relies on experience acquired during the organism's development, which includes gender socialization. Much of the variability in the wiring patterns of the brains of different individuals depends on the kinds of physical, social, and cultural environments they will encounter. It is not an exaggeration to say that "experience-dependent processes are central to understanding personality as a dynamic developmental construct that involves the collaboration of genetic and environmental influences across the lifespan" (Depue & Collins, 1999:507). Although brain plasticity is greatest in infancy and early childhood, a certain degree is maintained across the lifespan so that every time we experience or learn something we shape and reshape the nervous system in ways that could never have been genetically programmed. There are certainly arguments in neuroscience about brain developmental processes, but they are not about "*whether* the environment thoroughly influences brain development, but *how* it does" (Quartz & Segnowski, 1997:579; emphasis original).

Sex on the Brain

The strong social constructionist position is that masculinity and femininity is "all in the head," drummed into us by the social expectations of our socializing agents. The biosocial position also maintains that gender is "in our heads." It is bred into the brain's structure and function by eons of evolutionary selection pressures and then cultivated in different ways by the social expectations of a given time and place. In this chapter I go beyond the fundamental process of the brain's "sexing" of each of us as male or female to the more peripheral consequences of that sexing. Neuroscientists have made great strides in mapping numerous structural and functional differences in the brains of males and females, and we will examine sex-differentiated brain anatomy and physiology to the extent that they throw light on gender differences in criminal propensity. But a caveat is in order. While neurological data are certainly "harder" and more consistent than social science data, we have to be careful not to over-interpret them or to treat them as definitive.

According to neurobiologist Bruce Perry (2002:81), there are three key brain systems relevant to survival and reproductive success. They are mechanisms that (1) facilitate responses to threats to our well-being, (2) facilitate mate selection and reproduction, and (3) facilitate the protection and nurturing of the young. The mechanisms subserving these fitness concerns are dispersed throughout the brain and are of concern to both sexes. All three sets of mechanisms are present in both sexes because the roles these systems play are of concern to both sexes. Because some facets are more salient to one sex or the other, however, relevant brain structures and functions have evolved differently in males and females via sexual selection.

Brain Laterality

The most recent evolutionary addition to the brain is the cerebrum, which forms the bulk of the human brain. The cerebrum is divided into two complementary hemispheres which are connected at the bottom by the corpus callosum. It is generally accepted that the right hemisphere is specialized for perception, motor skills, spatial abilities, and the expression of emotion, and that the left hemisphere is specialized for language and analytical thinking (Parsons & Osherson, 2001). Female brains are less lateralized than male brains, which implies higher functional connectivity in female brains, that their cerebral hemispheres are less devoted to specialized tasks, and that both hemispheres contribute more equally to similar tasks than they do in males (Luders et al., 2006).

Testosterone (T) is strongly implicated in the process of lateralizing the brain. Chura and her colleagues (2010) find that increasing amounts of fetal T is significantly related to increasing rightward asymmetry of the corpus callosum in males. The fetal T in male brains slows down the maturation of the left hemisphere, thus allowing the right hemisphere to gain dominance. The lesser degree of lateralization in female brains means that there is more active cooperation between the hemispheres, which leads to better social cognitive processing. Neuroimaging studies show that women can more readily access and assess the rational and emotional content of social messages simultaneously as indexed by observed blood flow across the hemispheres (Lippa, 2003). It is known that the higher brain regions of the cerebrum (its outer layer, the cortex) develop sooner and faster in females, which explains their accelerated language development as well as the enhanced performance of males in right-hemisphere related visual-spatial tasks.

It is well established in neuroscience that higher IQ individuals have more efficient brains. Neural efficiency is typically tested via positron emission tomography (PET) scans which measure cerebral glucose metabolism as the brain takes up positron-emitting glucose applied to subjects by injection or inhalation. A computer reveals colorized biochemical maps of the brain identifying the parts activated while engaged in some task as the energy supplied by the glucose is metabolized. Glucose metabolic rates at various brain-slices (brain levels) have been correlated with IQ scores at between -.44 and -.84, which means that higher IQ persons expend less energy when performing intellectual tasks and possess brains that are speedier, more accurate, and more "energy efficient" than low IQ subjects (Gray & Thompson, 2004).

Interestingly, this inverse neural activation-intelligence relationship is moderated by gender. It holds for males when spatial tasks such as figure rotations are being performed and for females when a verbal matching task is performed and when identifying emotions in photographs (Jausovec & Jausovec, 2008). That is, higher IQ males expend less cerebral energy than lower IQ males when performing spatial tasks, and higher IQ females expend less than lower IQ females when performing verbal matching and emotional tasks. This phenomenon is interpreted as males having more efficient brains for visual-spatial tasks and females having more efficient brains for verbal and emotional tasks (Neubauer & Fink, 2009).

Male superiority in visual-spatial tasks and female superiority in verbal and object location memory is found in every culture where it has been tested. Silverman, Choi, and Peters (2007) examined data from almost 250,000 subjects in 40 countries and seven racial-ethnic groups and found this to be the case. They attribute these universals to the sexual division of labor during the Pleistocene era and beyond in which males were the primary hunters of meat and females the primary gatherers of plant food. Visual-spatial abilities have obvious utility in pursuing and hunting animals and then finding the way home at the conclusion of the hunt. On the other hand, object location memory and verbal skills are most useful in locating edible plants among a diversity of vegetation arrangements, remembering where that location is in the future, and communicating that fact to others.

We have briefly discussed hemispheric laterality because of its relationship to criminal behavior. In the absence of brain imaging technology, laterality may be indexed, albeit imperfectly, by discrepancy scores on the Wechsler IQ tests. Full-scale IQ scores are averages obtained by summing scores on verbal

(VIQ) and performance (PIQ) and then dividing by two. Most people have VIQ and PIQ scores that closely match, with a population average of 100 on each sub-scale. People who have either VIQ or PIQ subscale scores significantly in excess of the other (VIQ>PIQ or PIQ>VIQ) are considered intellectually imbalanced. Based on normative samples, a discrepancy of 12 points or more is considered a significant imbalance at the .01 level. From these samples 18% of American males are VIQ>PIQ imbalanced, 66% are balanced (VIQ=PIQ), and 16% are PIQ>VIQ imbalanced; for females the respective percentages were 15%, 66%, and 19% (Kaufman, 1976).

There are only insignificant differences between the genders today on verbal and performance IQ scores despite robust sex differences on other measures of verbal and visual-spatial abilities. This non-significance is designed into modern IQ tests. The initial Wechsler IQ tests did show highly significant sex differences between the sub-scales in the expected directions (females significantly greater VIQ; males significantly greater PIQ), but Wechsler wanted a sex-neutral measure of intelligence, not a measure of verbal and visual-spatial abilities per se. He achieved this by pruning the items on each subscale most responsible for the sex difference, thus today's items index verbal or performance skills less strongly than did the original items (Wells, 1980).[1]

Criminologists' interest in intellectual imbalance was first sparked by David Wechsler's (1958:176) statement that: "The most outstanding feature of the sociopath's test profile is the systematic high score on the performance as opposed to the verbal part of the scale." Subsequent research on the topic led Miller (1987:120) to remark that: "This PIQ>VIQ relationship was found across studies, despite variations in age, sex, race, setting, and form of the Wechsler scale administered, as well in differences in criteria for delinquency." Researchers consistently find that VIQ>PIQ imbalanced individuals are significantly *under*represented in criminal and delinquent populations, and that PIQ>VIQ individuals (females as well as males) are significantly *over*represented with an odds ratio of about 5.2 (Walsh, 2003). Because of Wechsler's pruning, intellectual imbalance cannot be used as an indicator of gender difference in criminal propensity because a PIQ>VIQ profile predicts female risk as well as male

---

1. While on the subject of intelligence, it is interesting to note that studies have found that gray matter is more correlated with IQ in men while in women IQ is more correlated with white matter. The brain's gray matter is composed of the neurons and their network of dendrites and includes the thin outer layer of the cerebral hemispheres (the cortex). White matter consists of the myelinated axons of the neurons. Myelin is the fatty sheath that coats the axons and enables them to conduct nerve impulses more rapidly.

risk (Walsh, 2003), but it does point to male-biased brain laterality as a fairly robust correlate of criminal behavior.

Arousal Levels

Reflective of evolutionary pressures directed at roles for child care and food gathering, females are more mindful of environmental stimuli—what is going on around them. This is demonstrated in numerous studies of memory of spatial configurations in which females consistently outperform males, such as the cross-cultural study by Silverman, Choi, and Peters (2007) discussed above.[2] Greater female attention to environmental details may reflect greater augmentation capabilities of the reticular activating system (RAS) in women. The RAS is a finger-sized bundle of neurons located at the core of the brain stem and feeds arousal stimuli to the thalamus for distribution throughout the brain. It is a sort of information filtering system that broadly determines consciousness, arousal and alertness. It has been suggested that females' greater attention to environmental stimuli may reflect an augmented RAS and also account for their lower rates of boredom proneness relative to males (Gemminggen, Sullivan, & Pomerantz, 2003), and why they are less prone to be sensation-seekers (Zuckerman, 2007).

Low cortical arousal and sensation seeking are both robustly linked to criminal behavior (Walsh & Ellis, 2007). Arousal theory is rooted on the common sense observation that people vary in their sensitivities and preferences for environmental stimulation. In identical environments some people are under aroused and others are over aroused, and both levels are psychologically uncomfortable. Most people are optimally aroused under the normal range of environmental conditions, but this level is stressful for some and boring for others (Raine, 1997). Individuals with overactive RASs are superoptimally aroused and seek to tone down environmental stimuli that most people find to be "just right" and quickly learn to avoid engaging in behavior that raises the intensity of stimuli to unpleasant levels. Such people are rarely found in criminal populations. Individuals with underactive RASs are suboptimally aroused

---

2. We should not confuse visual configuration abilities, which females excel in, with visual-spatial abilities, which males excel in. Visual configuration ability refers to such things as quickly identifying the form of something as determined by the arrangement of its parts, its color, or identifying matching items that enables classification of the thing perceived. Visual-spatial ability is the ability to visualize objects in space in one's mind, and how they could be viewed from a different perspective.

and bored with "just right" levels of stimulation and seek to boost stimuli to more comfortable levels. They require a high level of punishing stimuli before learning to avoid the behavior that provokes it, and are unusually prone to criminal behavior. A number of studies have shown that relative to the general population, criminals, especially those with the most serious records, are chronically under aroused as determined by electroencephalography (EEG) brain wave patterns, resting heart rate and skin conductance (Ellis, 2005).

Sensation seeking refers to the active desire for novel, varied, and extreme sensations and experiences often to the point of taking physical and social risks to obtain them. Sensation seekers with normal to above normal IQs and who are properly socialized will probably want to work as fire fighters, police officers, or any other job that provides physical activity, variety and excitement; low IQ and unsocialized individuals do not have those legitimate options available to them. A review by Ellis and Walsh (2000:219) found that 58 of 59 studies reported a statistically significant relationship between sensation seeking and various kinds of antisocial behavior.

Gender Biases in the Visual System

One of the perennial issues surrounding gender socialization is sex-linked toy and color preferences. These preferences have been used to argue both for the innateness of gender and for the power of socialization to mold gender. Recall the quote from Barrie Thorne (1993:2) in Chapter 6 in which she used color and toy preferences to argue that gender is social constructed via arbitrary societal norms: "Parents dress infant girls in pink and boys in blue, give them gender differentiated names and toys, and expect them to act differently." Toy preferences that are inconsistent with genital sex and assigned gender, such as observed by CAH girls and gender reassigned males, is an embarrassment to strong social constructionists, who put the inconsistency down to atypical gender socialization.[3] However, we see these sex differences in toy preferences at a very early age when children are allowed to choose and among non-human primates as well (Hines & Alexander, 2008); neither of these observations can reasonably be attributed to socialization.

It seems that there are strong innate biases for gender-typed toy preferences based on the influence of T (most likely the neonatal surge rather than fetal surge) on the visual pathways from the retina to image processing centers of the brain.

---

3. There is no evidence that CAH females receive "atypical" (i.e., male-typical) socialization. Indeed, because of their male-like behavior their parents often strive hard to socialize them in gender appropriate ways (Lippa, 2002).

There are a number of different types of cells that send visual information from the retina to the brain, with the two pertinent ones being parvocellular (P-cells) which are neurons that transmit information about the color and shape of stationary objects, and the magnocellular (M-cells) which carry information about depth and motion. Research consistently shows that females have significantly greater density of P-cells and males have significantly greater density of M-cells, which is consistent with the superior skill in the visual configuration ability to identify shape and color among females, and with males' superior visual-spatial skills in seeing motion and depth (Alexander, Wilcox, & Woods, 2009).

The evolutionary link is once again easy to discern here. As mentioned previously, female gatherers needed to recognize immobile plants by their shape and color (what it is) while male hunters needed to process the motion of prey or predator (where it is) to make a successful kill or to avoid being killed. Natural selection supplied the mechanisms to allow our ancestors to better perform their roles. These evolutionary mechanisms are reflected in today's gender-differentiated infant/child toy preferences. Boys' preference for moving objects such as toy trucks and balls is biased by their perceptual M-cells because these objects move in space and can be manipulated. Girls' preferences for dolls provide them opportunities to practice nurturance, and being more drawn to faces than moving objects is biased by the P-cell advantage (Alexander, 2003).

Some may argue that evolutionary explanations for gender-based color and toy preferences are "just so" stories. But there has to be some ultimate level explanation for why the P-cell/M-cell sexual dimorphism is present in contemporary human populations. As we have seen, it is common practice in biology to inquire into the fitness functions of any morphological, physiological, or behavioral trait that they observe in any animal species. Biologists consider this to be a crucial step in understanding the proximate functions of these traits. No one has come up with an alternative explanation for the observed sexual dimorphism in perceptual differences, which once again stresses how we can ill afford to ignore evolutionary theory in our thinking about gender. Natural selection seizes on and preserves whatever genetic variation is present in a population that will help organisms attend to their unconscious fitness concerns.

The Impact of Protracted Stress on Male and Female Brains

Stress is a state of psychophysiological arousal experienced when a challenge to our physical and/or mental well-being is perceived. Stress energizes and focuses us, and without it we would be seriously handicapped in our ability to meet life's challenges. Average levels of stress experienced during childhood inoculate us and calibrates our brains so that we may better navigate the travails of life. Adults who were protected from almost all stress during childhood are less well-equipped. While stress is functional, toxic and protracted stress does damage to vital brain areas responsible for memory storage and behavioral regulation such as the amygdala and the hippocampus. Childhood stressors that lead to frequent activation of stress response mechanisms may lead to the dysregulation of these mechanisms, leading to a number of psychological, emotional, and behavioral problems (Gunnar & Quevedo, 2007). The kinds of problems resulting from such stress may differ drastically according to gender.

The stress response is mediated by two separate but interrelated systems controlled by the hypothalamus: the autonomic nervous system (ANS) and the hypothalamic-pituitary-adrenal (HPA) axis. When we perceive a threat to our well-being, the hypothalamus directs the ANS's sympathetic branch to mobilize the body for vigorous action aided by pumping out the hormone epinephrine (adrenaline). When the threat is over the parasympathetic system restores the body to its previous range of set points (homeostasis). Protracted stress, however, can lead to a process known as allostasis, which describes the body's attainment of equilibrium by *altering* the acceptable range of physiological set-points to adapt to it rather than returning them to their previous state as in homeostasis. Physiological set-points can be either upwardly or downwardly deregulated.

The HPA axis response is slower than the ANS response and more protracted because it occurs through changes in gene expression (Gunnar & Quevedo, 2007). The HPA axis is activated in situations that call for a prolonged rumination rather than by the visceral immediacy of the ANS's fight or flight response. Part of the HPA axis response is the release of the hormone cortisol. Cortisol is the fuel that energizes our coping mechanisms by increasing vigilance and activity, and is therefore functional within the normal range. The brain is a major target for cortisol, and unlike epinephrine, cortisol is able to cross the blood/brain barrier (van Voorhees & Scarpa, 2004).

Frequent HPA axis arousal may lead to upward dysregulation of arousal mechanisms by the overproduction of cortisol, a condition known as *hypercortisolism*. Hypercortisolism leads to prolonged anxiety and depressive disorders and is most likely to be found in females who have been chronically stressed by being maltreated because females activate significantly more neural systems associated with emotional stress and with encoding it into long-term memory than males (van Voorhees & Scarpa, 2004). Females will thus have emotional experiences more readily available for rumination, and constant rumination increases their valence. Hypercortisolism suggests a failure of the system to adjust to chronic environmental stressors and leads to internalizing problems such as post traumatic stress disorder and depression (Hamann, 2005).

Chronically maltreated males, on the other hand, are likely to develop adaptive downward deregulation, or *hypocortisolism* (van Goozen et al., 2007). Downward regulation is adaptive because frequent stressful encounters habituate the organism to them such that it does not react to further encounters as it had previously and that both HPA axis and ANS response mechanisms have become blunted. Hypoarousal of the ANS and HPA axis is subjectively experienced as low levels of anxiety and fear, which is quite useful for those committing or contemplating a crime. Hypocortisolism has been linked to early onset of aggressive antisocial behavior (McBurnett et al., 2000) and to criminal behavior in general (Ellis, 2005). A study by O'Leary, Loney and Eckel (2007) found that males high in psychopathic traits lacked stress induced increases in cortisol displayed by males low in psychopathic traits. In short, the sex-differentiated stress response to chronic maltreatment provides further understanding about why the sexes/genders differ in criminal behavior—it leads to internalizing problems in females and externalizing problems, including crime, in males.

Chapter 11

Gender Differences in Prosocial Traits

Altruism

To understand a phenomenon it is wise to understand its opposite. If criminality has an opposite, it is altruism. Altruism is an active regard for the well-being of another; criminality is an active disregard for the well-being of just about everyone but one's self. As an active regard for others, altruism is a socially valued trait because it serves as a buffer against antisocial behavior, and thus it is no surprise that parents instinctively strive to cultivate it in their children. While it is true that humans (and all other sexually reproducing species) are necessarily born with a central concern for their own well-being, we are also born with altruistic tendencies that curb excesses and direct our self-concern in prosocial directions. Warneken and Tomasello (2009) explored multiple lines of human and non-human primate evidence pointing to the innateness of altruism. They show that altruistic tendencies emerge before socialization can have major effects, that later socialization is only effective if it meshes with the disposition to be altruistic, and that non-human primates display the same tendency absent socialization. They maintain that while socialization can build upon the natural predisposition to behave altruistically, it is not the source (also see Piliavin, 2009).

Given its importance in social life for its role in blunting antisocial impulses, it makes sense that altruism would exert pressure for selection. But altruism extends benefits to others at a cost to the altruist, so what evolutionary sense does it make for an organism to risk its own fitness to benefit others? Hamilton's (1964) theory of inclusive fitness (the direct fitness of the individual and the indirect fitness of its genetic kin) was one answer to this paradox, but this kind of altruism is exercised without any sort of conscious intentionality and is defined exclusively by its fitness consequences. Inclusive fitness and kin selection theories (the tendency to favor close genetic relatives over others) helps to explain how altruism could have been selected for in any species, but they are not satisfactory explanations for human altruism.

Acts in which an organism provides a benefit to another with an unconscious expectation of reciprocity—reciprocal altruism—has been offered as one explanation (Trivers, 1971). In hunter/gatherer bands, a hunter who has been successful and shares his meat with one who was not, extends a benefit to another at little cost to himself (his family cannot eat all the meat and it would soon spoil). The unspoken expectation is that if the tables are turned he and his family will be repaid in kind by the recipient of today's largesse. Because of the expectation of future reciprocity, reciprocal altruism is ultimately designed to benefit the altruist, and is thus not selfless, which fits it into evolutionary theory without resorting to group selectionism (Lehmann & Keller, 2006).

Altruism extended to non-kin in situations where reciprocity is unlikely is called "psychological altruism" (Kruger, 2003). We feel good when we extend some benefit to others without expectations of reciprocity; dropping money in a beggar's hat may make us feel superior, and giving to charitable causes may assuage any guilt we have about our privileged position. Psychological altruism is thus motivated by internal rewards (Brunero, 2002). We act altruistically because we feel good when we do, and because it confers valued social status on us by identifying us as persons who are kind, reliable, and trustworthy. In an evolutionary sense, we are altruists because our distant ancestors who were cooperative and giving enjoyed greater popularity among group members and reproductive success than those who were not, and the neural mechanisms that produce rewarding feelings when we do good things for others is the physiological adaptation.

A number of functional magnetic resonance imaging (fMRI) studies have shown that the same reward areas in the brain such as the ventral tegmental and stratium areas are activated whether giving or receiving something of value, but areas associated with social attachments and affiliation only "light up" when giving. The authors of one such study wrote in their conclusion that: "Taken together, these lines of evidence indicate that human altruism draws on general mammalian neural systems of reward, social attachment, and aversion. In the context of intertwined social and motivational contingencies, however, altruism tied to abstract moral beliefs relies on the uniquely developed human anterior prefrontal cortex" (Moll et al., 2009:15626). Sociological works have also shown that helping behavior such as volunteering has an apparent causal effect on volunteers' physical and psychological well-being (Pilliavin, 2009).

Individual organisms are adapted to act in fitness-enhancing ways, not to behave for the good of the group, but the individual's unconscious fitness goals are best realized by adhering to the rules of cooperation, and that is "for the good of the group." And, as we have just seen, multiple lines of evidence at-test to the fact that working for the good of the group is adaptive. Although the conscious intentions of altruists are other-oriented, actions are judged good or bad by natural selection according to their consequences, not by their inten-tions, That is, although intentional psychological altruism is ultimately (but un-consciously) self-serving, this does not diminish its value to its beneficiaries one bit. Selfishness as understood by biologists is both individually and socially desirable. It is by cooperating with others and being actively concerned with their well being (and others also behaving that way) that we simultaneously serve our own best interests and the best interests of our communities. This is quite different from selfishness as understood in the vernacular; i.e., the crabbed egotism of the antisocial individual shorn of any concern for others. This form of selfishness is ultimately self-defeating.

Geoffrey Miller (2007) focuses on sexual selection rather than natural selection (although the two are mutually reinforcing in this regard) to explain the evo-lution of altruism. He proposes that altruism and other moral virtues evolved to advertise genetic quality, parenting and partner qualities, fidelity, and kind-ness to potential mates. He states that the display of moral virtues "may sig-nal that a partner attaches positive utility to one's own happiness in addition to their own, which makes it much more likely that a Pareto-optimal [mutu-ally beneficial] equilibrium will be maintained in the relationship" (2007:101). Miller suggests that as *Homo sapiens* moved from male-centered intrasexual competition to female-centered epigamic sexual selection and to monogamous mating, females increasingly chose mates who signaled the willingness and ability to aid them in their fitness efforts. Males would also have become choosier about in whom they would invest their resources and look for the same moral virtues. Altruistic signals thus became both individually and cul-turally valued in a process of gene-culture coevolution (what genetic poly-morphisms are useful to fitness concerns in this culture at this time).

Gender Differences in Altruism

There are large differences among individuals in levels of altruism. One of the largest behavior genetic studies of altruism (as measured by self-reports) reported a heritability coefficient of .56 for the trait, which was roughly sim-ilar when calculated separately for men and women (Rushton et al., 1986). However, an evolutionary perspective rooted in parental investment theory would strongly predict that females would be more altruistic toward their chil-dren than males and that this tendency would spread to include others. Mothers are always certain of their maternity, but paternal certainly is always a question mark. Cross-culturally, it has been estimated that males express low levels of paternal certainty in 45% of pre-industrial societies (Eswaran & Kotwal, 2004). In modern societies, it has been roughly determined that between 1% and 20% (depending on socioeconomic settings) of children are not the children of the putative father (Geary, Vigil, & Byrd-Craven, 2004). As a result of paternal uncertainty, males tend to curtail their investment in their putative offspring because the fitness payoff for cuckolds is zero.

Socialization theories would also predict that mothers would invest more (be more altruistic) in their children than fathers because women are socialized to be more nurturing and to maintain familial relationships. Following this logic they would predict that both sets of grandmothers would invest more than both sets of grandfathers, and that the ordering from most to least in grandmotherly and grandfatherly solicitude would be more or less arbitrary. However, the cross-cultural literature is unequivocal in its findings on the matter: The ordering of grandparent solicitude is maternal grandmother, maternal *grandfather*, paternal grandmother, paternal grandfather (reviewed in Michalski & Shackleford, 2005). Again, the Darwinian interpretation of this ordering would be the relative parental certainty subconsciously presumed by maternal grandparents (Laham, Gonsalkorale & von Hippel, 2005).

The evidence relating to which gender is more altruistic in a more general sense comes from many kinds of studies such as self-reports, observational field work, experiments, and neuroimaging studies. This body of literature, almost without exception, shows that females are more altruistic than males. Using experimental economic methods, Andreoni and Vesterlund (2001) found that when altruism is cheap, men were more altruistic, but when it was more costly, women were more altruistic. Piper and Schnepf's (2008) analysis of charitable giving in Great Britain revealed that after controlling for personal income and marital status, women donated significantly more money than men. Interestingly, women's giving was focused more on nurture-related charities such as animal, children, and elderly welfare, while men's giving was more focused on religious organizations. Yamasue and colleague's (2008) fMRI study of 155 Japanese subjects showed that the higher measured cooperativeness of females relative to males was tightly coupled with gray matter volume in the various frontal cortices. These authors concluded that: "The present findings suggest that genetic factors coding development of the social brain [the PFC] influence altruistic cooperativeness more directly in females" (2008:2337). The next issue is why females are more altruistic, and thus more prosocial and less criminal.

Empathy

Altruistic behavior requires some sort of cognitive process to motivate it, but cognition requires emotional guidance as much as emotion requires rational guidance (Richter-levin, 2004). Frans de Waal (2008) maintains that the more evolutionarily distant emotional trait of empathy channels altruism in social species because it does not rely on cognitive ruminations about such things as reciprocity concerns. Empathy is the cognitive and emotional ability to understand the feelings and distress of others as if they were our own. The cognitive component allows us to understand why they are feeling distress, and the emotional component allows us to "feel" it with them. To the extent that we feel empathy for others, we have an evolved visceral motivation to take some action to alleviate their distress if we are able. Emotions per se cannot enhance fitness; there has to be a behavior associated with the internal states to give them selective potency. Altruism can be thought of as the co-evolved behavioral component of empathy. The basis of empathy is the distress we feel personally when witnessing the distress of others, and if we can alleviate the distress of others we thereby alleviate our own. Thus, empathy also has a selfish component submerged below consciousness. It is a very good thing that it does because we call people who lack emotional connectedness to others psychopaths, and such people are callously indifferent to the needs and suffering of others.

Frans de Waal (2008) posits that empathy is an ancient phylogenic capacity predating the emergence of *Homo sapiens* which evolved rapidly in the context of mammalian parental care.[1] Empathy is an integral component of the love and nurturing of offspring because caregivers must quickly and automatically relate to the distress signals of their offspring. Given that offspring care is primarily (in evolutionary times, overwhelmingly) maternal, selection pressures for empathy would have operated more strongly in females than in males. Parents who were not alerted to or were unaffected by their offspring's distress signals or by their smiles and cooing are surely not among our ancestors. This is another example of an adaption leading to enhanced fitness of the individual and also something that is highly valued by the group. Like the diffusion of adaptive love and nurturance of genetic offspring to the non-adaptive love

---

1. This is supported by evidence that oxytocin, which is only present in mammals, has survived an estimated 700 million years with few modifications. Oxytocin's precursor, vasotocin, controls sexual behavior and birthing in reptiles that provide the absolute minimal or no maternal care to offspring. Oxytocin appears to be vital for mammals, especially for mammals such as humans who have extremely altricial offspring (MacDonald & MacDonald, 2010).

and nurturance of the children of others and to pets, the capacity for empathetic responses, once locked into the human repertoire, diffused to a wider network of social relationships.

What is it that allows us to link the self-other relationship in empathetic responses? There has to be some neural architecture that gives rise to shared representation of affective states. Neuroscientists have located the ability in so-called mirror neurons. Mirror neurons are brain cells that fire (respond) equally whether an actor performs an action or witnesses someone else performing the action. Thus, the neuron "mirrors" the behavior of another as though the observer were acting in the same way. It is not simply a matter of being cognitively aware of the actor ("Jane is upset"); it is the actual firing of *identical* neurons in the observer's brain that are firing in the brain of the person being observed. This neuron mimicry operates outside of the observer's conscious awareness. It is assumed that this unconscious communication between neurons of one person and another reflects a correspondence between self and other that turns an observation into empathy. The human mirror neuron system (hMNS) is distributed throughout motor areas of the brain and the sub-cortices of the PFC.

The cognitive aspects of hMNS's role in helping us to gain access to someone else's thoughts and feelings can be though of as the physiological mechanism governing the psychologists' "theory of mind" (ToM) or the sociologists' concept of "taking the role of the other." Both require that a person distinguish between the self and other and that he or she can use his or her own mind to infer the feelings, thoughts, intentions, and desires of others. We might say that the ability to identify with others is the portal for empathy. It has been shown in fMRI studies that mirror neuron mechanisms are selectively recruited when attributing feelings to the self or to others in response to viewing a variety of emotional facial expressions (angry, fearful, sad, etc.). Moreover, subjects with higher empathy scores on a variety of empathy scales show stronger brain activation, particularly in the various frontal cortices (Schulte-Ruther et al., 2007).

Gender Differences in Empathy

As with altruism, there are large individual differences in empathy. The estimated heritability of empathy is .68 and is roughly the same for both genders (Rushton et al., 1986) but, females are invariably found to more empathetic than males regardless of the tools and methods used to assess it (Campbell, 2006). This difference may be traced to the effects of fetal testosterone (T)

(Knickmeyer et al., 2006), and/or to higher oxytocin (OT) functioning in females (Taylor, 2006), and ultimately to sex-differentiated natural selection for
nurturing behavior. The "male" hormone T acts antagonistically to the "female" peptide OT, which both supports the observation that females empathize
more strongly than males, and the notion that the evolution of empathy was
driven by caregiving (Herman, Putman, & van Honk, 2006). A study of 20
healthy females who received either a single sublingual dose of T or a placebo
showed that the T administered group showed a significant reduction in empathetic responses to experimental stimuli (Hermans, Putman, & van Honk,
2006). Conversely, a study of 30 healthy males by Domes and his colleagues (2007)
showed that a single intranasal dose of OT significantly enhanced their ability
to infer the mental states of others relative to a placebo control group. An fMRI
double-bind study of 15 healthy males (Kirsch et al., 2005) showed that a single intranasal dose of OT significantly reduced amygdala activity in response
to angry faces and threatening scenarios relative to subjects receiving a placebo.
Thus males become more empathetic with the administration of OT, and females become less so with the administration of T. All these responses took
place outside conscious awareness because the brain target sites for both T and
OT are located in the limbic system.

Another fMRI study comparing neural correlates of empathy and gender
differences found that females recruit far more emotion-related brain areas
than males, particularly bilateral amygdala activation ($r = -.525$) when processing empathy-related stimuli (Derntl et al., 2010). Males tended to recruit
neural networks associated with cognitive evaluation rather than emotional
evaluation. The researchers also found that females who were in the follicle
stage of the menstrual cycle were more empathetic than women not in that
phase (the amygdalae have high concentrations of hormone receptors that
modulate their activity). Derntl and her colleagues (2010) speculated increased
social sensitivity to social cues during this phase would have increased our ancestral females' mating chances during times of increased fertility.

Females tend to be better than males in reading or "mirroring" the emotions of others as shown in neuroscience studies of the hMNS using a variety
of techniques. One fMRI study concluded that "females recruit areas containing mirror neurons to a higher degree than males during both self- and other-
related processing in empathetic face-to-face interactions" (Schulte-Ruther et
al., 2008:393). Supporting evidence comes from EEG studies of mu rhythm
activity, which is the result of sensorimotor neurons spontaneously firing at a
particular frequency. Mu waves are one of the wave forms defined by fre-
quencies (Hertz Hz), amplitude, and shape. They are detected by electroencephalography picking up electrical activity in the brain. The higher the Hz

the greater the measured brain activity (alertness), with beta waves (> 13Hz) having the highest frequency and delta (3 Hz or less) the lowest. Mu waves are in the alpha wave range (8–13 Hz) and are blocked when a person performs some motor act *or* when watching some other person perform the same act (Chang et al., 2008). The extent to which the EEG detects mu blockage in a person's brain is the extent to which mirror neurons are being activated. EEG studies show that individuals scoring higher on empathy scales suppress the mu rhythm to a greater degree than those scoring lower, and that females suppress mu more strongly than males (Cheng et al., 2008). Multiple lines of evidence thus lead to the conclusion that, as evolutionary theory would predict, females are on average far more empathetic than males.[2]

Guilt Proneness

Guilt is an important self-regulatory emotion that involves anxiety, remorse, and concern about how one's actions have negatively impacted others. It is a socially adaptive form of moral affect that motivates both avoidance and approach behavior. Because guilt is psychologically punitive, it motivates one not to repeat the transgression (avoidance), and because it also moves one toward reparative behavior (apologies, restitution, etc.) it motivates approach behavior. As we might expect, guilt is positively related to empathy since persons are not likely to feel bad about offending others if they are indifferent to them (Silfver & Klaus, 2007). Females show higher overall levels of guilt-proneness than males whether assessed via self-reports — and often very strongly so — (Silfver et al., 2008), or PFC activity recorded by EEGs (Amodio, Devine, & Harmon-Jones, 2007).

Females are more guilt-prone than males about most, but not all, transgressions. Females are more likely to feel guilty for expressing angry aggression or for inconsiderate behavior, which is predictable both from their higher

---

2. The use of the phrase "on average" leads us away from that nasty essentialist label. There are some men higher on empathy than the average woman, and some women lower than the average man. One way of quantifying gender differences in empathy is scores on Baron-Cohen's (2003) empathy quotient (EQ) scale which is often used as a correlate of brain areas and brain activity in brain imaging-recording studies. Effect sizes (Cohen's d) in four studies reviewed in Nettle (2007) were .63, .76, .86, and .89. Because d is expressed in terms of standard deviation units, it is equivalent to a z score, which is equivalent to an area under the normal curve. Taking the weighted average of these ds (.80), we have an area under the normal curve of about .79. The intuitive interpretation is that 79% of women (or about 4 out of 5) score higher on the EQ scale than the average man.

levels of empathy and from the fact that such behavior is in violation of gender roles. Sex differences in guilt are less in evidence in young children but become more pronounced with age (Bennett, Farrington, & Huesmann, 2005). In short, guilt focuses a person's thoughts on recognizing the rights of others and their duty to respect that. This inner voice is conspicuously absent or greatly attenuated in criminals and less developed in males in general. Thus we have yet another reason for suspecting a priori that women would offend less than men.

Conscientiousness and Agreeableness

Conscientiousness and agreeableness are two other prosocial traits which numerous studies show the genders to be significantly different. Conscientiousness includes a number of sub-traits such as disciplined, scrupulous, orderly, responsible, and reliable at one end of the continuum, and careless, unreliable, irresponsible, and unscrupulous at the other (Lodi-Smith & Roberts, 2007). Agreeableness is the tendency to be friendly, considerate, courteous, helpful, and cooperative with others, all indicating a high degree of concern for prosocial conformity and social desirability. Disagreeable persons display the opposite characteristics—suspicious, unfriendly, uncooperative, and unhelpful—which suggest a lack of concern for prosocial conformity and social desirability. Conscientiousness has a mean estimated heritability of .49 (Bouchard et al., 2003) and agreeableness an estimate of .48 (Jang et al., 1998). Conscientiousness and agreeableness are positively correlated (Witt et al., 2002), but far from perfectly. One can be conscientious at work but thoroughly disagreeable socially (think of the Machiavellian white-collar crook), and one can be agreeable socially but lackadaisical at work (think of the ritualist of anomie theory).

We do not expect the average criminal to score very well on these two traits, as Miller and Lynam's (2001:780) description of the typical criminal attests:

> Individuals who commit crimes tend to be hostile, self-centered, spiteful, jealous, and indifferent to others (i.e., low in Agreeableness). They tend to lack ambition, motivation, and perseverance, have difficulty controlling their impulses, and hold nontraditional and unconventional values and beliefs (i.e., are low in Conscientiousness).

Miller and Lynam's meta-analysis compared 29 prisoner/non-prisoner samples found significant negative correlations between agreeableness and substance abuse (-.30), antisocial behavior (-.32), and aggression (-.56), and weaker significant correlations between conscientiousness and antisocial behavior (-.19) and aggression (-.15). Jacobwitz and Eagan (2006) found that agreeableness was significantly related to primary psychopathy (-.43), secondary psychopathy (-.23), Machiavellianism (-.41) and narcissism (-.43). In the Coasta et al. (2001) and Schmitt et al. (2008) studies of personality in cultures around the world discussed in Chapter 4, higher levels of both agreeableness and conscientiousness were reported by females relative to males in almost all of them. The biggest gender differences in conscientiousness and agreeableness were found in the most egalitarian and economically developed societies in both studies.

Chapter 12

Gender Differences in Major Risk Factors for Criminality

Impulsiveness/Low Constraint/ Low Self-Control

Although impulsiveness, low constraint, and low self-control are somewhat different constructs, they are similar enough to be treated as one construct. All three involve disinhibited behavior in which the actor is unable or unwilling to consider the long-term consequences of his or her behavior (Chapple & Johnson, 2007). These constructs also contain elements of risk taking and sensation seeking. The authors of a meta-analysis of self-control studies that included close to 50,000 subjects concluded that it is "one of the strongest known correlates of crime" (Pratt & Cullen, 2000:952).

Humans learn to control their impulsive reactions to temptation and to aggressive responses to provocation via two interrelated inhibition routes. The first route is entirely visceral in nature (sympathetic ANS arousal) and is called *reactive inhibition*. Reactive inhibition is fear-based and automatically impels attention to threats and initiates avoidance/withdrawal behavior in response. The second system is called *effortful control*. With the increasing ability to think before acting, effortful control develops on the superstructure of reactive inhibition and reflects the increased role of the socialization process. Effortful control allows for reflection on the long-term negative consequences of a contemplated behavior, such as avoiding an opportunity to steal even though there are no possible immediate negative consequences because contemplating the theft evokes thoughts of possible long-term consequences. Behavioral inhibition is thus more a function of visceral fear (harm avoidance) than other more cognitive components of inhibition such as guilt and embarrassment (Driscoll et al., 2006).

Because females are less vulnerable to a range of brain insults than males, and because reactive inhibition has more valence for them (see discussion of fear in Chapter 8), they are better able to exercise effortful control over their behavior (Bennett, Farrington, & Huesmann, 2005). Males may engage in more impulsive behavior because testosterone not only creates sexually dimorphic brains in utero, it also appears to inhibit synaptic pruning in adolescent males (Paus et al., 2010).[1] Whether it be a function of reactive or effortful control (again, these mechanisms are not mutually exclusive—the former strongly affects the later), females have, *without exception*, showed greater levels of constraint/self-control across numerous studies regardless of differences in data, methods, culture, or ages of subjects (Chapple & Johnson, 2007).

ADHD: Definitions and Prevalence

Attention-deficit/hyperactivity disorder (ADHD) is defined clinically in the American Psychiatric Association's (APA, 1994) Diagnostic and Statistical Manual of Mental Disorders (DSM-IV) as a disruptive behavior disorder characterized by ongoing inattention and/or hyperactivity-impulsivity occurring in several settings more frequently and severely than is typical for persons at the same stage of development. Three major types of ADHD have been recognized: The inattentive type (unorganized, difficulty following instructions, easily distracted); the hyperactive-impulsive type (constantly in motion, restless, impulsive, difficulty in following directions), and the combined type in which the symptoms of the first two types are equally in evidence.

ADHD is the most commonly diagnosed behavioral disorder of young children and adolescents and it is strongly related to delinquent and criminal behavior (Ellis & Walsh, 2000). Gudjonsson and colleague's (2009) review of nine studies of prevalence rates of ADHD among adult prison inmates in a number of countries using various diagnostic criteria found rates ranging from 24% to 67%, with their own study showing that 62.5% of inmates were either fully ADHD symptomatic or in partial remission. These figures are extremely high given estimated prevalence in the general population of between 4% and 10%. The traits manifested by ADHD individuals associated with criminal behavior include impairment of executive functions, low self-control, low arousal levels, difficulty with peers, disruptive behavior, academic underachievement, risk taking, and proneness to extreme boredom.

---

1. Synaptic pruning is a regulatory weeding out process by which "strong" synaptic connections between brain cells (connections that have been frequently strongly connected in response to environmental events with significant emotional content) are retained while "weak" ones are eliminated. This process is very active during adolescence and leads to a more efficient synaptic configuration as the brain slowly matures to its adult state.

The Genetics and Neurobiology of ADHD

Heritability estimates for ADHD average .80 and are consistently found regardless of whether it is considered a categorical or continuous trait (Bobb et al., 2006). Molecular genetic studies show ADHD to be highly polygenic, with at least 50 genes with small to moderate effects being involved (Comings et al, 2005). The highly polygenic nature of ADHD probably explains why it is so clinically heterogeneous and why it is linked to many other problems such as conduct disorder (CD), substance abuse, pathological gambling, and antisocial behavior in general. The three genetic polymorphisms that meta-analyses (Bobb et al., 2006; Gizer, Ficks, & Waldman, 2009) show the most replicated are the dopamine receptor D4 (DRD4), the dopamine transporter (DAT1), and the serotonin transporter (5-HTT). The 5-HTT and the DAT1 alleles have been found to be associated with criminality in national representative samples (Vaughn et al., 2009).[2]

Dopamine is a powerful regulator of behavioral and cognitive functions, thus any aspect of reduced dopaminergic functioning results in behavioral and cognitive dysregulation. Both the 7 repeat allele of the DRD4 and the 10 repeat allele of the DAT1 are associated with reduced dopaminergic functioning (Mill et al., 2006). Dopamine motivates us to seek pleasurable stimuli, but too much of a good thing can lead to addiction to the pleasures being sought. If dopamine is the accelerator of behavior, serotonin is the brake. The 5-HTT transports serotonin back to the vesicles in the presynaptic knob terminating its activity, and one variant of the 5-HTT more rapidly clears serotonin from the synapse resulting in its reduced availability of the behavior-inhibiting "brake" (Wallis et al., 2008).

ADHD and CD Comorbidity

In addition to placing individuals at increased risk for antisocial behavior, delinquents with ADHD are more likely than non-ADHD delinquents to persist in their offending as adults. This probability rises dramatically for ADHD individuals who are comorbid for CD. CD is a neurological disorder with heritability estimates ranging between .27 and .78 (Coolidge, Thede, & Young, 2000). CD is defined as persistent serious antisocial acts (assault, stealing, setting fires, bullying, vandalism) that are excessive for a child's developmental stage,

---

2. See note 1, Chapter 8 for a description of genetic polymorphisms.

and is considered one of the most stable diagnoses in psychiatry (Comings et al., 2005). Lynam (196:209) has stated that the ADHD+CD combination is a "particularly virulent strain…. best described as fledgling psychopathy." ADHD and CD are found to co-occur in about 50% of cases in most clinical and epidemiological studies (Waschbusch et al., 2002).

Moffitt et al. (1994) propose that verbal deficits place children at risk for CD. This gains some support from a study of children comorbid for ADHD and reading disorder which showed that both were caused in part by common genetic effects (Friedman et al., 2003). Neurological evidence suggests that the left frontal lobes contain the mechanisms by which children process their parents' instructions and which become their internalized basis of self-control. Children with deficits in these mechanisms fail to profit from their parent's verbal instructions and tend to develop a present-oriented and impulsive cognitive style. Lacking normal ability to connect abstract verbal commands with their own concrete behavior, such children may have to learn lessons through the more painful process of trial and error and may thus experience more frequent punishments for their lack of compliance in a process of G x E interaction that exacerbates antisocial conduct.

Gender Differences in ADHD and CD

Males are significantly more likely to be diagnosed with ADHD than females. The male-female ratio is largest for the combined type (7.3:1), followed by the hyperactive-impulsive type (4:1), and lowest for the inattentive type (2.7:1) (Rhee & Waldman, 2004). Conduct disorder has an onset at around five years of age and remains at a steady rate for girls (about 0.8%) and rises to about 2.8% at age 15, but rises steadily in boys from about 2.1% at age five to about 5.5% at age 15 (Maughan et al., 2004). As opposed to the typical male ADHD + CD comorbidity, females with ADHD tend to be comorbid for internalizing disorders such as depression and anxiety rather than CD (Sasi, 2010).

The serotonergic system is a strong candidate for helping us to understand gender differences in ADHD behavior. Neuroimaging studies report significant sex differences in serotonin receptor and transporter binding sites in the brain (e.g., Jovanovic et al., 2007), and estrogen is known to increase certain serotonin receptor and transporter sites (Verona & Vitale, 2006). The relationship between low serotonin and impulsive violent behavior is consistently found, and is "perhaps the most reliable findings in the history of psychiatry" (Fishbein, 2001:15). A good deal of research has shown that males and females react differently to reductions in serotonin functioning. One such experimental study using a technique called "acute tryptophan depletion," a process that rapidly decreases serotonin levels in the brain, found that men became more impulsive and women became more cautious with lowered serotonin (Walderhaug et al., 2008). Women also reported a worsening of their mood, but men did not report any mood changes.

Alcoholism

The American Medical Association defines alcoholism as "a primary, chronic disease characterized by impaired control over drinking, preoccupation with the drug alcohol, use of alcohol despite adverse consequences, and distortions in thinking" (Morse & Flavin, 1992:1012). Of all drugs, alcohol has the closest association with crime. It is estimated that one-third of all arrests (excluding DUI) in the United States are for alcohol-related offenses, that about 75% of robberies and 80% of homicides involve a drunken offender and/or victim (Schmalleger, 2006), and about 40% of other violent offenders in the United States had been drinking at the time of the offense (Martin, 2001).

Alcohol is at once the most deadly and the most popular of our chemical comforters because it boosts confidence and loosens social inhibitions at social gatherings. Although alcohol is ultimately a brain-numbing depressant, at low dosage levels it is a stimulant because it raises dopamine levels (Ruden, 1997). Alcohol also initially increases serotonin, but then rapidly decreases it, resulting in reducing the impulse control capacity of the PFC (Badawy, 2003). It also reduces anxiety and tension by affecting the neurotransmitter gamma-aminobutyric acid (GABA), which is a major inhibitor of neuron excitation (Buck & Finn, 2000).

Given the strong relationship between alcohol and criminal behavior, it is reasonable to suppose that both have some common cause. This is not to imply that alcoholism and criminality are synonymous. Researchers have divided alcoholics broadly into *Type I* and *Type II* alcoholics. Type II alcoholics start drinking (and using other drugs) at a very early age and rapidly become addicted, and have many character disorders and behavioral problems that *precede* their alcoholism. Type I alcoholics start drinking later in life and progress to alcoholism slowly. Type Is typically have families and jobs, and any character defects they may have are typically induced by the alcohol and are not permanent (Crabbe, 2002). Fishbein (1998) proposes that Type II alcoholics have inherited abnormalities of the serotonin and dopamine systems that may be driving both their drinking and their antisocial behavior. It has also been shown that Type IIs, but not Type Is, tend to have PFC deficits (Oscar-Berman et al., 2009).

Research increasingly shows that vulnerability to alcohol addiction is strongly genetic (Slaught, Lyman, & Lyman, 2004). Various estimates of the heritability of alcoholism range between 0.49 and 0.64 for both sexes (Nayak et al., 2008). For Type II alone, heritability is about 0.90 and less than 0.40 for Type I alcoholism (McGue, 1999). There are a bewildering number of genes that make and control neurotransmitters and enzymes implicated in alcoholism. A meta-analysis of 2,343 lines of evidence identified 316 alcohol addiction-related genes and 13 addiction-related pathways (the molecular routes and interactions among neurotransmitters and enzymes to produce the effect) to alcohol addiction (Li, Mao, & Wei, 2008).

Gender Differences in Alcoholism

According to the Substance Abuse and Mental Health Services Administration (Morse & Flavin, 2007), males (10.5%) are about twice as likely as females (5.1%) to meet the criteria for alcohol dependence or abuse in the general population. The overall heritability of alcoholism is similar for both genders, but as Crabbe (2002:449, emphasis added) describes the distinction between the two types of alcoholism: "Type I alcoholism is characterized by mild abuse, minimal criminality, and passive-dependent personality variables, whereas Type II alcoholism is characterized by early onset, violence, and criminality, *and is largely limited to males.*" Nayak and his colleagues (2008) also claim that Type II alcoholism is limited to males, although there is always danger in claiming gender exclusivity for any trait or syndrome. However, a study of 48 alcoholic murderers in Germany did find that while there was an equal number of male and female Type I (8 and 8) alcoholic murderers, all 32 Type II alcoholic murderers were males (Reulbach et al., 2007).

Disorders such as alcoholism are typically associated with other disorders. The sex differences underlying alcoholic types may be a function of different patterns, of comorbidity; i.e., the sexes may differ in the mechanisms associated with the comorbidity of alcoholism and other disorders. As Prescott (2002:269) explains: "Male and female alcoholics differ in their patterns of comorbidity, with women having higher rates of comorbid anxiety and affective disorders and males having higher rates of comorbid use of other drugs, conduct disorder, and antisocial personality disorder." These different patterns have different risk levels for criminal behavior attached to them.

Psychopathy

Psychopathy is a personality disorder characterized by amoral conduct facilitated by fearlessness, callousness, and a lack of empathy. Psychopaths come from all social and cultural backgrounds, are superficially charming and glib, have normal intelligence, and can function perfectly normally (if not morally) in society. They are excellent mimics of normal human emotion, and because they do not exhibit any signs of guilt, embarrassment, or shame, they are able to manipulate others with relative ease. Psychopaths are probably what Cesare Lombroso had in mind with his "morally insane" category of born criminals; i.e., those "who appear normal in physique and intelligence but cannot distinguish good from evil" (cited in Gibson, 2002:25).

Leading researchers in this area assert that psychopaths constitute a small group of individuals whose numbers remain fairly stable across cultures and time periods, that they can come from any social class or racial or ethnic group, and that the syndrome is biological in origin. Psychopathy is a personality disorder consisting of a cluster of traits such as insensitivity to other's feelings, self-absorbed, conscienceless, relatively fearless, impulsive, no capacity for love, and a promiscuous sex life. If we were to sum up these traits with a single word, it would be hard to find a better one than *emotionless*.

The "gold standard" for the assessment of psychopathy used in prisons worldwide is Robert Hare's Psychopathy Checklist-Revised (PLC-R). Scores on the PCL-R range from zero to 40, with 30 being the cutoff score for a diagnosis of psychopathy. Factor analysis of the PCL-R reveals that psychopathy is comprised of two factors, one describing a constellation of personality traits that point to insensitivity to the feelings of others, and the second a generally unstable, impulsive, and deviant lifestyle. While the traits associated with these factors sometimes exist independently, both are often present in the same individuals. It is frequently found that the physiological and neurological anomalies associated with psychopathy correlate with high scores on factor 1 (personality traits) but not necessarily with factor 2 (unstable and antisocial lifestyle), and that low IQ correlates with high scores on factor 2, but not on factor 1 (Harris, Skilling, & Rice, 2001; Patrick, 1994). Psychopaths who are successful entrepreneurs, CEOs, cult leaders, military men, and politicians may exploit and manipulate others but may never commit any violation of the penal code, and will score high on factor 1 but not on factor 2.

The stability of the prevalence of psychopaths over time and their existence across class lines has led to the virtual dismissal of environmental causes of psychopathy by those most engaged in this line of research (Kinner, 2003; Pitchford, 2001). As Robert Hare, the world's foremost psychopathy researcher

(1993:170) remarks: "I can find no convincing evidence that psychopathy is the direct result of early social or environmental factors." This does not mean that such factors are irrelevant to understanding psychopathic *behavior*. The alleged lack of environmental effects is belied by Waldman and Rhee's (2006) meta-analysis of behavior genetic studies of psychopathy which found an average heritability of .49 and a non-shared environment effect of .51 (no variance was accounted for by shared environment). However, all the studies included in the meta-analysis used self-reported psychopathy measures from community samples; none used the PCL-R, and environmental effects seem to be limited to factor 2 scores (Verona & Vitale, 2006).[3]

Psychopathy and the Social Emotions

If psychopathy is primarily genetic there must be a number of identifiable physiological markers that distinguish them from non-psychopaths. The greatly reduced ability to experience the social emotions of shame, embarrassment, guilt, empathy, and love has marked psychopaths across time and cultures. The social emotions are distinguished from the primary emotions such as anger and joy, and have evolved as integral parts of our social lives. They serve to provide clues about the kinds of relationships that we are likely to have with others (cooperative vs. uncooperative) and serve as "commitment devices" and "guarantors of threats and promises" (Mealey, 1995:525). Barkow (1989:121) describes them as involuntary "limbic system overrides" that serve to adjust our behavior in social situations. Social emotions focus and modify brain activity to move us to behave in ways that enhanced our distant ancestor's reproductive success by overriding decisions suggesting alternatives to cooperation that may have been more rational in the short term, but fitness reducing in the long term (Walsh, 2006). These feelings arising in the limbic system prevent us from doing things that might be to our immediate advantage (steal, lie, cheat) but would cost us in reputation and future positive relationships.

---

3. The lack of consensus over whether or not environmental factors affect the development of psychopathy has led to conceptual confusion and drift. Psychopathy, sociopathy, and antisocial personality disorder (ASPD) are often used interchangeably, but they are relatively distinct concepts. Psychopathy may be almost entirely genetic in origin; the development of sociopathy (mostly individuals high on factor 2) would include strong environmental input, and ASPD is a definition that would fit criminal psychopaths and sociopaths, although it is flawed as a scientific concept because its definition is constrained by legalities; i.e., it is a psychiatric/legal term that depends to some extent on age and criminal history (Walsh & Wu, 2008).

The positive and negative feelings we experience when we survey the possible consequences of our actions keep most of us on the straight and narrow most of the time. The weaker we feel them, the more likely we are to exploit others, the stronger we feel them, the less likely we are to exploit others. This is the emotional component of our consciences coming into play.

Numerous researchers have studied emotional responses in psychopaths compared to non-psychopaths using brain wave patterns measured via the EEG. For instance, researchers may present psychopaths and non-psychopaths with a list of emotionally neutral and emotionally laden words and compare their brain wave responses. With emotionally neutral words (cup, apple) both psychopaths and the non-psychopaths show a small spike in their brain waves indicating that they have recognized the word. When non-psychopaths are presented with emotionally laden words (cancer, death, mom) there is a much larger spike indicating that they have recognized the word and made associations that have led to pairing the cognition with emotions. When psychopaths are presented with those same emotional words, they tend to process them in ways similar to processing neutral words. That is, recognize it and pass on to the next word without involving the emotions. Hundreds of other studies using many different kinds of methods have revealed over and over that the defining characteristic of psychopaths is their inability to "tie" the brain's cognitive and emotional networks together (Levenson et al., 2000, Scarpa & Raine, 2003). A burgeoning neuroimaging literature has identified numerous cortical (e.g., PFC) and subcortical (e.g., amygdala) deficits associated with psychopathy (see Blair, 2006 and Raine & Yang, 2006 for reviews). As noted earlier, emotional deficits are primarily related to PCL-R factor I psychopaths.

Richard Wiebe (2004:33) sums up the literature on emotional processing of psychopaths as follows: "Unlike non-psychopaths, psychopaths tend not to react autonomically to either faces or words that convey emotions. Further, they do not recognize fear and disgust as readily, although they can identify other basic emotions. These features allow the psychopath to cold-bloodedly pursue selfish interests, without being distracted by emotional signals, especially the fear and disgust of another person." Wiebe reminds us that the defining traits of chronic offenders evolved not for the purposes of any act we now call criminal, but for successful mating efforts. Because chronic cheats operate "below the emotional poverty line" (Hare, 1993:134), they do not reveal physical clues that would allow others to judge their intentions. Lacking an emotional basis for self-regulation, chronic cheats make social decisions exclusively on the basis of rational calculations of immediate costs or benefits.

The low fear hypothesis advanced by Lykken (1995; 2006) is another explanation for psychopathy based on a trait that strongly differentiates the genders. Lykken writes: "Like the ability to experience pain, the fear mechanism is especially useful early in life before the individual's judgment and reason are sufficiently dependable guides to behavior" (1995:144). Fear and anxiety are emotional components of the conscience, the strength of which has a lot to do with the ANS's typical level of arousal (van Bokhoven, et al., 2005). Lykken's premise is that psychopaths are difficult to condition because they are relatively fearless, and that they are relatively fearless because they have ANSs that are hypoarousable. A low fear quotient can account for psychopaths' lack of social emotions that enable them to cheat and manipulate others because it makes it difficult to visualize the negative aspects of impending events, much of which relies on emotional processing. In other words, psychopaths have a tendency to take risks that most of us would rather avoid because of the negative consequences associated with them.

Gender Differences in Psychopathy

It has been estimated that between one and three percent of the male population and less than one percent of the female population are psychopaths (Pitchford, 2001), although psychopaths make up about 20 percent of the American prison population (Wiebe, 2004). On a dimensional scale, Cale and Lilienfeld (2002) describe self-report studies based on the Psychopathic Personality Inventory (PPI), which contains such subscales as Machiavellian egocentricity, cold heartedness, fearlessness, impulsiveness, and stress immunity. A Cohen's d of .97 was found for sex differences in PPI scores averaged across all subscales, with males scoring significantly higher on all subscales. An effect size of .97 is intuitively interpreted as approximately 83% of males (just over 4 out of 5) scoring higher than the average female (see note 2, Chapter 11). In a college sample and using the screen version of the PCL-R, Hart, Cox, and Hare (1995) found that males scored significantly higher with effect sizes of .96 for factor 1 and .74 for factor 2.

As with ADHD and alcoholism, female psychopaths display different co-morbidity and patterns of symptoms than males. For instance, Warren et al.'s (2005) study of female criminals found that their PCL-R scores were correlated only with crimes typically associated with women such as property crimes and prostitution and not with crimes of violence as they are with males. Similarly, Verona and Vitale's (2006) review of the literature found that disorders most commonly diagnosed in females such as borderline personality disorder, histrionic personality disorder, and somatization disorder tend to represent female expressions of psychopathy as opposed to such things as sadism and violent aggression that often represents male psychopathy. In terms of antiso-cial externalizing behaviors of female psychopaths, they list prostitution, abuse and neglect of offspring, intimate partner violence, and "relational forms of ag-gression such as friendship betrayal and 'backbiting' " (2006:431). The point is that even when clinically diagnosed with the label that represents the quintes-sential criminal, female psychopaths exhibit less serious forms of criminal be-havior than their male counterparts.

General Conclusion

The overall conclusion of this book is that cross cultural, evolutionary, hor-monal, genetic, and neurological data all converge on the conclusion that we should strongly *expect* to see the low rate of criminal offending among females relative to males. There is certainly no mystery about it; the gender ratio prob-lem is really only a problem for those who refuse to look at the biosocial whole of human behavior. Indeed, a profound mystery would exist if we actually found a culture in which we *did not* find large sex differences in antisocial behavior of all kinds. If there were no deep biological differences between the sexes we would see some cultures in which female rates were close to or even surpassed male rates since socialization practices alone would account for gendered behavior. Because no such culture has ever existed, it is nothing less than scientific malfea-sance to cling to an explanation that cannot possibly be sustained.

The perverse refusal to turn to the more advanced sciences for guidance can only be explained by either ignorance or ideology. Ignorance is easily rectified by learning aspects of these sciences that are pertinent to our interests. Crim-inologists cannot expect to be experts in all of these relevant areas, or even in one of them. All we have to do is learn the fundamentals of these sciences just as we learn the fundamentals of statistics to conduct quantitative research with-out becoming mathematical statisticians. Ideology is the deeper river we have to forge. Recall Cooper, Walsh, and Ellis' (2010) study in Chapter 7 in which 24 different theories were listed by 379 American criminologists as enjoying the most empirical support. Self-reported ideology (conservative, moderate, liberal and radical) was by far the best predictor of favored theory, with con-servatives and moderates opting for more individual-type theories such as self-control, and liberals and radicals opting for structural-type theories such as social disorganization (only 3 out of 379 selected feminism, all three were women self-identified as liberal or radical).

This situation reminds us of Thomas Sowell's (1987) constrained and un-constrained "visions." The constrained vision views human activities as constrained by an innate human nature that is largely unalterable. The unconstrained vision denies an innate human nature and believes that it is perfectible. The many differences between the two visions are summed up by the constrained vision's assertion that: "this is how the world *is*," and the unconstrained vision's assertion that: "this is how the world *should be*." Traditional feminist criminologists have a vision about what *should* be (legal, social, political, and economic equality between the sexes), which is a moral judgment with which I completely agree. But criminology is struggling to be a science and thus cannot content itself with conclusions that precede its inquiries. Gaining gender justice does not depend on the fiction of the lack of biological differences between the sexes/genders. The sexes come into this world with many differences forged over eons of evolutionary history that lead to different levels of antisocial behavior; this is an empirical "is," not a moral "should" or "should not." That this empirical fact, supported by literally thousands of lines of evidence, upset so many feminist apple carts is something of a mystery. Sex differences are something to celebrate, and acknowledging them should not be seen as an impediment to the social justice goals of feminism; not acknowledging them, however, is a clear impediment to the goals of feminist criminology.

If forced to boil down the proximate foundational reasons for the universal sex difference in criminal behavior to their bare minimum, it would have to be sex differences in empathy and fear. Empathy and fear are the natural enemies of crime for fairly obvious reasons. Empathy is other oriented and prevents one from committing acts injurious to others because one has an emotional and cognitive investment in the well being of others. Fear is self-oriented and prevents one from committing acts injurious to others out of fear of the consequences to one's self. Many other prosocial tendencies flow from these two basic foundations, such as a strong conscience, altruism, self-control, and agreeableness. As we have seen, sex-differentiated levels of empathy and fear have evolved in response to sex-differentiated reproductive roles of males and females. Empathy assured the rapid identification and provision of infant needs, and nourished social relationships. Fear kept both mother and child out of harm's way and provided a sturdy scaffold around which to build a conscience. Again, there is considerable gender overlap in these and other traits associated with pro- and anti-social behavior, but robust average sex differences in them are always found.

The advantages to be gained by feminist criminologists by understanding behavior as evolutionary biologists, neurobiologists, and geneticists do are a legion. Criminology can ill afford to remain oblivious to the robust and consistent evidence coming from mature sciences if it is ever to reach maturity itself. Socialization is the important process that turns our raw biological beings into civilized social beings, but we must come to terms with what biology will allow our socialization practices to accomplish. Socialization practices have their place in our explanations of behavioral variation, but like the drunk who knew he hadn't lost his keys under the lamppost but perversely continued looking there anyway "because that's where the light is," criminologists who refuse to look anywhere else are fooling themselves without the excuse of inebriation. To put it more bluntly, if we continue to call upon differential gender socialization as our only explanation for gender differences in criminal behavior, we will go nowhere except into scientific oblivion. We must realize that gender socialization rests on the solid bedrock of sex differentiated biology forged by countless thousands of years of contrasting sexual selection pressures.

References

Adler, F. (1975). *Sisters in Crime: The Rise of the New Female Criminal*. New York: McGraw-Hill.

Akers, R. & C. Sellers (2009). *Criminological theories: Introduction, evaluation, and application* (5th ed.). New York: Oxford University Press.

Alcock, J. (2001). *The triumph of sociobiology*. New York: Oxford University Press.

Alexander, G. (2003). An evolutionary perspective on sex-typed toy preferences: Pink, blue, and the brain. *Archives of Sexual Behavior*, 32:7–14.

Alexander, G., T. Wilcox, & R. Woods (2009). Sex differences in infants' visual interest in toys. *Archives of Sexual Behavior*, 38:427–433.

Allen, C. (2007). It's a boy! Gender expectations intrude on the study of sex determination. *DNA and Cell Biology*, 26:699–705.

American Psychiatric Association (1994). *Diagnostic and statistical manual of mental disorder* (4th ed.). Washington, DC: American Psychiatric Association.

Amodio, D., P. Devine & E. Harmon-Jones (2007). A dynamic model of guilt: Implications for motivation and self-regulation in the context of prejudice. *Psychological Science*, 18:524–530.

Anderson, E. (1994). The code of the streets. *The Atlantic Monthly*, 5:81–94.

Anderson, E. (1999). *Code of the street: Decency, violence, and the moral life of the inner city*. New York: W.W. Norton.

Andreoni, J. & L. Vesterlund (2001). Which is the fair sex? Gender differences in altruism. *The Quarterly Journal of Economics*, 115:293–312.

Andersson, M. & L. Simmons (2006). Sexual selection and mate choice. *Trends in Ecology and Evolution*, 21:296–302.

Aron, A., H. Fisher, D. Mashek, G. Strong, H. Li, & L. Brown (2005). Reward, motivation, and emotion systems associated with early-stage intense romantic love. *Journal of Neurophysiology*, 94:327–337.

Arnold, A. (2004). Sex chromosomes and brain gender. *Nature Reviews: Neuroscience*, 5:1–8.

Arnold, A., J. Xu, W. Grisham, X. Chen, & Y. Kim (2009). Minireview: Sex chromosomes and brain differentiation. *Endocrinology*, 145:1057–1062.

Badawy, A. (2003). Alcohol and violence and the possible role of serotonin. *Criminal Behaviour and Mental Health*, 13:31–44.

Badcock, C. (2000). *Evolutionary psychology: A critical introduction.* Cambridge, England: Polity Press.

Barak, G. (1998). *Integrating criminologies.* Boston: Allyn & Bacon.

Barkow, J. (1989). Darwin, sex and status: Biological approaches to mind and culture. Toronto: University of Toronto Press.

Barkow, J. (1992). Beneath new culture is an old psychology: Gossip and social stratification. In Barkow, J., L. Cosmides, & J. Tooby (Eds.). *The Adapted mind: evolutionary psychology and the generation of culture.* (pp. 627–637). New York: Oxford University Press.

Baron-Cohen (2003). *The essential difference: The truth about the male and female brain.* New York: Basic Books.

Barrett, H. (2001). On the functional origins of essentialism. *Mind & Society*, 2:1–30.

Bartels, A. & S. Zeki (2004). The neural correlates of maternal and romantic love. NeuroImage, 21:1155–1166.

Bateman, P. & N. Bennett (2006). The biology of human sexuality: Evolution. ecology, and physicology, *Verbum et Ecclesia*, 27:245–264.

Bates, K., C. Bader, & F. Menchen (2003). Family structure, power-control theory and deviance: Extending power-control theory to include alternate family forms. *Western Criminology Review*, 4:170–190.

Beaver, K., J. Wright, & A. Walsh (2008). A gene-based Evolutionary explanation for the association between criminal involvement and number of sex partners. *Biodemography and Social Biology*, 54:47–55.

Belsky, J. & P. Draper (1991). Childhood experience, interpersonal development, and reproductive strategy: An evolutionary theory of socialization. *Child Development*, 62:647–670.

Bennett, S., D. Farrington, & L. Huesman (2005). Explaining gender differences in crime and violence: The importance of social cognitive skills. *Aggression and Violent Behavior*, 10:263–288.

Bernard, T., J. Snipes, & A. Gerould (2010). Vold's theoretical criminology. New York: Oxford University Press.

Betzig, L. (1999). When women win. *Behavioral and Brain Sciences*, 22:217.

Blair, R. (2006). Subcortical brain systems in psychopathy: The amygdala and associated structures. In C. Patrick (Ed.), *Handbook of psychopathy*, pp. 297–312. New York: The Guilford Press.

Bobb, A., F. Castellanos, A. Addington, & J. Rapoport (2005). Molecular genetic studies of ADHD: 1991 to 2004, *American Journal of Medical Genetics—Neuropsychiatric Genetics*, 132:109–125.

Bohan, J. (1993). Regarding gender: Essentialism, constructionism, and feminist psychology. *Psychology of Women Quarterly*, 17:5–21.

Bouchard, T. (2004). Genetic influence on human psychological traits: A survey. *Current Directions in Psychological Science*, 13:148–151.

Bouchard, T., N. Segal, A. Tellegen, M. McGue, M. Keyes, & R. Krueger (2003). Evidence for the construct validity and heritability of the Wilson-Patterson conservatism scale: A reared-apart twins study of social attitudes. *Personality and Individual Differences*, 34:959–969.

Boyle, M. (1990). *Schizophrenia: A scientific delusion*. London: Routledge.

Bradley, S., G. Oliver, A. Chernick, & K. Zucker (1998). Experiment of nurture: Ablatio penis at 2 months, sex reassignment at 7 months, and a psychosexual follow-up in young adulthood. *Pediatrics*, 102, 91–95.

Brebner, J. (2003). Gender and emotions. *Personality and Individual Differences* 34:387–394.

Briken, P., N. Habermann, W. Berner, & A. Hill (2006). XYY chromosome abnormality in sexual homicide perpetrators. *American Journal of Medical Genetics*, 141b:198–200.

Bromage, T. (1987). The biological and chronological maturation of early hominids. *Journal of Human Evolution*, 16-257–272.

Brown, D. (1991). *Human universals*. New York: McGraw-Hill.

Brunero, J. (2002). Evolution, altruism and internal reward explanations. *Philosophical Forum*, 33:413–424.

Byrnes, J., D. Miller, & W. Schafer (1999). Gender differences in risk taking: A meta-analysis. *Psychological Bulletin*, 125:367–383.

Buck, K. & D. Finn (2000). Genetic factors in addiction: QTL mapping and candidate gene studies implicate GABAergic genes in alcohol and barbiturate withdrawal in mice. *Addiction*, 96:139–149.

Buss, D. (2005). *The murderer next door: Why the mind is designed to kill*. New York: Penguin.

Byne, W. (2006). Developmental endocrine influences on gender identity. *The Mount Sinai Journal of Medicine*, 73:950–959.

Cahill, L., N. Uncapher, L. Kilpatrick, M. Alkire, & J. Turner (2004). Sex-related hemispheric lateralization of amygdala function in emotionally-influenced memory: An fMRI investigation. *Learning and Memory*, 11:261–266.

Cale, E. & S. Lilienfeld (2002). Sex differences in psychopathy and antisocial personality disorder: A review and integration. *Clinical Psychology Review*, 22:1179–1207.

Campbell, A. (1999). Staying alive: Evolution, culture, and women's intrasexual aggression. *Behavioral and Brian Sciences*, 22:203–214.

Campbell, A. (2006a). Feminism and evolutionary psychology. In J. Barkow (Ed.), *Missing the revolution: Darwinism for social scientists*, pp. 63–99. Oxford: Oxford University Press.

Campbell, A. (2006b). Sex differences in direct aggression: What are the psychological mediators? *Aggression and Violent Behavior*, 6:481–497.

Campbell, A. (2008). Attachment, aggression and affiliation: The role of oxytocin in female social behavior. *Biological Psychology*, 77:1–10.

Campbell, A. (2009). Gender and crime: An evolutionary perspective. In A. Walsh & K. Beaver (Eds.), *Criminology and Biology: New directions in theory and research*. pp. 117–136. New York: Routledge.

Campbell, A., S. Muncer, & D. Bibel (2001). Women and crime: An evolutionary approach. *Aggression and Violent Behavior*, 6:481–497.

Campbell, A., L. Shirley, & J. Candy (2004). A longitudinal study of gender-related cognition and behaviour. *Developmental Science*, 7:1–9.

Canli, T., J. Desmond, Z. Zhao, & J. Gabrieli (2002). Sex differences in the neural basis of emotional memories. *Proceedings of the National Academy of Sciences*, 99:10789–10794.

Carlen, P. (1983). *Women's imprisonment: A study in social control*. London: Roudedge and Kegan Paul.

Carey, G. (2003). *Human genetics for the social sciences*. Thousand Oaks, CA: Sage.

Cashdan, E. (1993). Attracting mates: Effects of parental investment on mate attraction strategies. *Ethology and Sociobiology*, 14:1–23.

Cartwright, J. (2000). *Evolution and Human Behavior*. Cambridge, MA: MIT Press.

Chapple, C. & K. Johnson (2007). Gender differences in impulsivity. *Youth Violence and Juvenile Justice*, 5:221–234.

Chauncey, G., N. Cott, J. D'Emilio, E. Freedman, T. Holt, J. Howard, L. Hunt, M. Jordan, E. Kennedy, & L. Kerber (2003). Amicus brief of history professors in the matter of *John Geddes Lawrence and Tyron Garner v. State of Texas*. On line at www.findlaw.com.

Cheng, Y., P. Lee, C-Y. Yang, C-Y. Lin, D. Hung, & J. Decety (2008). Gender differences in the mu rhythm of the human mirror-neuron system. *PloS One*, 3:e2113.

Chesney-Lind, M. (1995). Girls, delinquency and juvenile justice: Toward a feminist theory of young women's crime. In B. Price & N. Sokoloff (Eds.), *The criminal justice system and women: Offenders, victims, and workers* (pp. 71–88). New York: McGraw-Hill.

Chesney-Lind, M. (2006). Patriarchy, crime, and justice: Feminist criminology in an era of backlash. *Feminist Criminology*, 1:6:26.

Chesney-Lind, M. & R. Sheldon, (1992). *Girl's delinquency and juvenile justice.* Pacific Grove, CA: Brooks/Cole.

Chura, L., M. Lombardo, E. Ashwin, B. Auyeung, B. Chakrabarti, E. Bullmore, & S. Baron-Cohen (2010). Organizational effects of fetal testosterone on human corpus callosum size and asymmetry. *Psychoneuroendocrinology,* 35:122–132.

Cloward, R. & L. Ohlin (1960). *Delinquency and opportunity.* New York: Free Press.

Cohen, A. (1955). *Delinquent boys.* New York: Free Press.

Comings, D., T. Chen, K. Blum, J. Mengucci, S. Blum, & B. Meshkin (2005). Neurogenic interactions and aberrant behavioral co-morbidity of attention deficit hyperactivity disorder (ADHD): Dispelling myths. *Theoretical Biology & Medical Modeling,* 2:50:65.

Connell, R. & J. Messerschmidt (2005). Hegemonic masculinity: Rethinking the concept. *Gender and Society,* 19:829–859.

Coolidge, F., L. Thede, & S. Young (2000). Heritability and the comorbidity of attention deficit hyperactivity disorder with behavioral disorders and executive function deficits: A preliminary investigation. *Developmental Neuropsychology,* 17:273–287.

Cooper, J., A. Walsh, & L. Ellis (2010). Is Criminology Ripe for a Paradigm Shift? Evidence from a Survey of American Criminologists. *Journal of Criminal Justice Education.*

Costa, P., A. Terracciano, & R. McCrae (2001). Gender differences in personality traits across cultures: Robust and surprising findings. *Journal of Personality and Social Psychology,* 81:322–331.

Crabbe, J. (2002). Genetic contributions to addiction. *Annual Review of Psychology,* 53:435–462.

Craig, I., E. Harper, & C. Loat (2004). The genetic basis for sex differences in human behaviour: Role of sex chromosomes. *Annals of Human Genetics,* 68:269–284.

Cronin, H. (2003). Getting human nature right. In Brockman, J, (ed.) *The new humanist: science at the edge,* pp. 53–65. New York: Barnes & Noble.

Cullen, F. (2009). Foreword to A. Walsh & K. Beaver, *Biosocial Criminology: New directions in theory and research.* New York: Routledge.

Daly, K. & M. Chesney-Lind (1988). Feminism and criminology. *Justice Quarterly,* 5:497–538.

Daly, M. & M. Wilson (2001). Risk-taking, intersexual competition, and homicide. *Nebraska Symposium on Motivation,* 47:1–36.

Davies, A. & T. Shackleford (2008). Two human natures: How men and women evolved different psychologies. In By C. Crawford & D. Krebs

(Eds.), *Foundations of evolutionary psychology*, pp. 261–281. Danvers, MA: CRC Press.

DeLisi, L., A. Maurizo, C. Svetina, B. Ardekani, K. Szulc, J. Nierenburg, J. Leonard, & P. Harvey (2005). Klinefelter's syndrome (XXY) as genetic model for psychotic disorders. *American Journal of Medical Genetics*, 135:15–23.

Dennett, D. (1995). *Darwin's Dangerous Idea: Evolution and the Meanings of Life*. New York: Simon & Schuster.

Depue, R. & P. Collins (1999). Neurobiology of the structure of personality: Dopamine, facilitation of incentive motivation, and extraversion. *Behavioral and Brain Sciences*, 22:491–569.

Derntl, B., A. Finkelmayer, S. Eickhoff, T. Kellerman, D. Falkenberg, F. Schnieder, & U. Habel (2010). Multidimensional assessment of empathetic abilities: Neural correlates and gender differences. *Psychoneuroendocrinology*, 35:67–82.

deVries, G. & P. Sodersten (2009). Sex differences in the brain: The relation between structure and function. *Hormones and Behavior*. 55:589–596.

de Waal, F. (2008). Putting the altruism back into altruism: The evolution of empathy. *Annual Review of Psychology*, 59:279–300.

Diamond, M. (1999). Pediatric management of ambiguous and traumatized genitalia. *The Journal of Urology*, 162:1021–1028.

Domes, G., M. Heinrichs, A. Michel, C. Berger, & S. Herpertz (2007). Oxytocin improves "mind-reading" in humans. *Biological Psychiatry*, 61:731–733.

Driscoll, H., A. Zinkivskay, K. Evans, & A. Campbell (2006). Gender differences in social representations of aggression: The phenomenological experience of differences in inhibitory control. *British Journal of Psychology*, 97:139–153.

Dunbar, R. (2007). Male and female brain evolution is subject to contrasting selection pressures in primates. *BioMedCentral Biology*, 5:1–3.

Dunbar, R. & S. Shultz (2007). Evolution of the social brain. *Science*, 317:1344–1347.

Edelman, G. (1992). *Bright air, brilliant fire*. New York: Basic Books.

Ehrenreich, B & J. McIntosh (1997). The new creationism: Biology under attack, *The Nation*, 9:12–16.

Ellis, L. (2005). A theory explaining biological correlates of criminality. *European Journal of Criminology*, 2:287–315.

Ellis, L. & J. McDonald (2001). Crime, delinquency, and social status: A reconsideration. *Journal of Offender Rehabilitation*, 32:23–52.

Ellis, L. & A. Walsh (2000). *Criminology: A global perspective*. Boston: Allyn & Bacon.

Engels, F. (1884/1988). Engels on the origin and evolution of the family. *Population and Development Review*, 14:705–729. Originally published as *The origin of the family, private property, and the state.*

Esch, T. & G. Stefano (2005). Love promotes health. *Neuroendocrinology Letters*, 3:264–267.

Eswaran, M. & A. Kotwal (2004). A theory of gender differences in parental altruism. *Canadian Journal of Economics*, 37:918–950.

Evans, P., S. Gilbert, N. Mekel-Bobrov, E. Vallender, J. Anderson, L. Vaez-Azizi, S. Tishkoff, R. Hudson, & B. Lahn (2005). *Microcephalin*, a Gene Regulating Brain Size, Continues to Evolve Adaptively in Humans. *Science*, 309:1717–1720.

Fausto-Sterling, A. (2002). Gender identification and assignment in Intersex Children. *Dialogues in Pediatric Urology* 25:4–5.

Fetchenhauer, D. & B. Buunk (2005). How to explain gender differences in fear of crime: Towards an evolutionary approach. *Sexualities, Evolution and gender.* 7:95–113.

Fishbein, D. (1992). The psychobiology of female aggression. *Criminal Justice and Behavior*, 19:99–126.

Fishbein, D. (1998). Differential susceptibility to comorbid drug abuse and violence. *Journal of Drug Issues*, 28:859–891.

Fishbein, D. (2001). *Biobehavioral perspectives in criminology*. Belmont, CA: Wadsworth.

Flavin, J. (2001). Feminism for the mainstream criminologist: An invitation. *Journal of Criminal Justice*, 29:271–285.

Fortune, W. (1939). Apapesh warfare. *American Anthropologist*, 41:22–41.

Friedman, M., N. Chabildas, N., Budhiraja, E. Willcutt, & B. Pennington, B.F. (2003). Etiology of the comorbidity between reading disability and ADHD: Exploration of the non-random mating hypothesis. *American Journal of Medical Genetics Part B (Neuropsychiatric genetics)*, 120b:109–115.

Garrett, B. (2009). *Brain and behavior: Introduction to biological psychology*. Los Angeles: Sage.

Geary, D. (2000). Evolution and proximate expression of human paternal investment. *Psychological Bulletin*, 126:55–77.

Geary, D. (2005). *The origin of mind: Evolution of brain, cognition, and general intelligence*. Washington, DC: American Psychological Association.

Geary, D. & M. Flinn (2002). Sex differences in behavioral and hormonal response to social threat: Commentary on Taylor et al (2000). *Psychological Review*, 109:745–750.

Geary, D., J. Vigil, & J. Byrd-Craven (2004). Evolution of human mate choice. *The Journal of Sex Research*, 41:27–42.

Gemmingen, M., B. Sullivan, & A. Pomerantz (2003). Investigating the relationships between boredom proneness, paranoia, and self-consciousness. *Personality and Individual Differences*, 34:907–919.

Gewertz, D. (1981). A historical reconsideration of female dominance among the Chambri of Papua New Guinea. *American Ethnologist*, 8:94–106.

Gewertz, D. & Errington, F. (1991). *Twisted Histories, Altered Contexts: Representing the Chambuli in a World System*. Cambridge: Cambridge University Press.

Gibson, M. (2002). *Born to crime: Cesare Lombroso and the origins of biological criminology*. Westport, CT: Praeger.

Gintis, H. (2003). The hitchhiker's guide to altruism: Gene-culture coevolution and the internalization of norms. *Journal of Theoretical Biology*, 220:407–418.

Gizer, I., C. Ficks, & I. Waldman (2009). Candidate gene studies of ADHD: A meta-Analytic review. *Human Genetics*, 126:51–90.

Glueck, S. & E. Glueck (1934). *Five hundred delinquent women*. New York: Knopf.

Goldberg, E. (2001). *The executive brain: Frontal lobes and the civilized mind*. New York: Oxford University Press.

Goldberg, S. (1986). Utopian yearning versus scientific curiosity. *Society*, 23:29–39.

Gooren, L. (2006). The biology of human psychosexual development. *Hormones and Behavior*, 50:589–601.

Goos, L. & I. Silverman (2001). The influence of genomic imprinting on brain development and behavior. *Evolution and Human Behavior*, 22:385–407.

Gottfredson, M. & T. Hirschi (1990). A general theory of crime. Stanford: Stanford University Press.

Gray, J. & P. Thompson (2004). Neurobiology of intelligence: Science and ethics. *Nature Reviews: Neuroscience*, 5:471–482.

Grusec, J. & P. Hastings (eds.) (2007). Introduction. *Handbook of socialization: Theory and research*, pp. 1–9. New York: Guilford Press.

Gudjonsson, G, J. Sigurdsson, S. Young, A. Newton & M. Peersen (2009). Attention deficit hyperactivity disorder (ADHD). How do ADHD symptoms relate to personality among prisoners? *Personality and Individual Differences*, 47:64–68.

Gunnar, M. & K. Quevedo (2007). The neurobiology of stress and development. *Annual Review of Psychology*, 58:145–173.

Gur, R. C, F. Gunning-Dixon, W. Bilker, & R. E. Gur (2002). Sex differences in temporo-limbic and frontal brain volumes of healthy adults. *Cerebral Cortex*, 12:998–1003.

Hacking, I. (2006). Genetics, biosocial groups & the future of identity. *Daedalus*, 135:81–95.

Hagan, J. (1989). *Structural criminology*. New Brunswick, NJ: Rutgers University Press.

Hagan, J. (1990). The structuration of gender and deviance: A power-control theory of vulnerability to crime and the search for deviant role exits. The *Canadian Review of Sociology and Anthropology*, 27:137–56.

Hamilton, W. (1964). The evolution of social behavior. *Journal of Theoretical Biology*, 7:1–52.

Hamann, S. (2005). Sex differences in the responses of the human amygdala. *The Neuroscientist*, 11:288–293.

Hare, R. (1993). *Without conscience: The disturbing world of the psychopaths among us*. New York: Pocket books.

Harpending, H. & P. Draper (1988). Antisocial behavior and the other side of cultural evolution. In T. Moffitt, & S. Mednick (Eds.), *Biological contributions to crime causation*, pp. 293–307. Dordrecht: Martinus Nyhoff.

Harris, G., T. Skilling, & M. Rice (2001). The construct of psychopathy. In M. Tonry (Ed.), *Crime and justice: A review of research*, pp. 197–264. Chicago: University of Chicago Press.

Hart, S., D. Cox, & R. Hare (1995). The Hare psychopathy checklist: Screening version, Multi-Health Systems, Toronto, ON.

Hawks, J., E. Wang, G. Cochran, H. Harpending, & R. Moyzis (2007). Recent acceleration of human adaptive evolution. *Proceedings of the National Academy of Science*, 104:20753–20758.

Heimer, K. & S. De Coster (1999). The gendering of violent delinquency. *Criminology*, 37:277–318.

Hepper, P. (2005). Unravelling our beginnings. *The Psychologists*, 18:474–477.

Hermans, E., P. Putman, & J. van Honk, (2006). Testosterone reduces empathetic mimicking in healthy young women. *Psychoneuroendocrinology*, 31, 859–866.

Hines, M. (2004). *Brain gender*. Oxford: Oxford University Press.

Hines, M. (2006). Prenatal testosterone and gender-related behavior. *European Journal of Endocrinology*, 155:115–121.

Hines, M. & G. Alexander (2008). Monkeys, girls, boys and toys: a confirmation Letter regarding "Sex differences in toy preferences: striking parallels between monkeys and humans." *Hormones and Behavior*, 54:359–364.

Hines M., S. Golombok, J. Rust, K. Johnston, J. Golding, & The Avon Longitudinal Study of Parents and Children Study Team (2002). Testosterone during pregnancy and gender role behavior of preschool children: a longitudinal, population study. *Child Development*, 73:1678–1687.

Hopcroft, R. (2009). Gender inequality in interaction: An evolutionary account. *Social Forces*, 87:1845–1872.

Hryb, D., A. Nakhla, S. Kahn, J. St. George, N. Levey, N. Romas, & W. Rosner (2002). Sex hormone-binding globulin in the human prostate is locally synthesized and may act as an autocrine/paracrine effector. *Journal of Biological Chemistry*, 277:26618–26622.

Huber, J. (2008). Reproductive biology, technology, and gender inequality: An autobiographical essay. *Annual Review of Sociology*, 34:1–13.

Hublin, J. & H. Coqueugniot (2006). Absolute or proportional brain size: That is the question. *Journal of Human Evolution*, 50:109–113.

Hunnicutt, G. & L. Broidy (2004). Liberation and economic marginalization: A reformulation and test of (formerly?) competing models. *Journal of Research in Crime and Delinquency*, 41:130–155.

Irwin, K. & M. Chesney-Lind (2008). Girls' violence: Beyond dangerous masculinity. *Sociology Compass*, 2/3:837–855.

Jafee, S., T. Moffitt, A. Caspi, & A. Taylor (2003). Life with (or without) father: The benefits of living with two biological parents depend on the father's antisocial behavior. *Child Development*, 74:109–126.

Jang, K., R. McCrae, A. Angleitner, R. Riemann, & W. Livesley (1998). Heritability of facet-level traits in a cross-cultural twin sample: support for a hierarchical model of personality. *Journal of personality and social psychology*, 74:1556–65.

Jausovec, N. & K. Jausovec (2008). Spatial rotation and recognizing emotions: Gender related differences in brain activity. *Intelligence*, 36:383–393.

Jovanovic, H., J. Lundberg, P. Karlsson, Å. Cerin, T. Saijo, A.Varrone, C. Halldin & A. Nordström (2008). Sex differences in the serotonin 1A receptor and serotonin transporter binding in the human brain measured by PET. *NeuroImage*, 39:1408–1419.

Jung, R., C. Gasarovic, R. Chavez, A. Caprihan, R. Barrow, & R. Yeo (2009). Imagining intelligence with proton magnetic resonance spectroscopy. *Intelligence*, 37:192–198.

Jurgensen, M., O. Hiort, P. Holterhus, & U. Thyen (2007). Gender role behavior in children with XY karyotype and disorders of sex development. *Hormones and Behavior*, 51:443–453.

Kanazawa, S. (2003). A general evolutionary psychological theory of criminality and related male-typical behavior. In Walsh, A. & L. Ellis (Eds.). *Biosocial criminology: Challenging environmentalism's supremacy*, pp. 37–60. Hauppauge, NY: Nova Science.

Kaufman, A. (1976). Verbal-performance IQ discrepancies on the WISC-R. *Journal of Consulting and Clinical Psychology*, 44:739–744.

Kennair, L. (2002). Evolutionary psychology: An emerging integrative perspective within the science and practice of psychology. *The Human Nature Review*, 2:17–61.

Kennelly, I., S. Mertz, & J. Lorber (2001). What is gender? *American Sociological Review*, 66:598–605.

Kimura, D. (1992). Sex differences in the brain. *Scientific American*, 267:119–125.

Kinner, S. (2003). Psychopathy as an adaptation: Implications for society and social policy. In R. Bloom & N. Dass (Eds.), *Evolutionary psychology and violence*, pp. 57–81. Westport, CT: Praeger.

Kirsch P., C. Esslinger, Q. Chen, D. Mier, S. Lis, S. Siddhanti, H. Gruppe, V. Mattay B. Gallhofer, & A. Meyer-Lindenberg (2005). Oxytocin modulates neural circuitry for social cognition and fear in humans, *Journal of Neuroscience*, 25:11489–11493.

Klein, D. (1995). The etiology of female crime: A review of the literature. In B. Price & N. Sokoloff (Eds.), *The criminal justice system and women: Offenders, victims, and workers* (pp. 30–53). New York: McGraw-Hill.

Knafo, A., A. Iervolino, & R. Plomin (2005). Masculine girls and feminine boys: genetic and environmental contributions to atypical gender development in early childhood. *Journal of Personality and Social Psychology*. 88:400–412.

Knickmeyer, R., S. Baron-Cohen, P. Raggatt, K. Taylor, & G. Hackett (2006). Fetal Testosterone and empathy. *Hormones and Behavior*, 49:282–292.

Kochanska, G. & A. Knaack (2003). Effortful control as a personality characteristic of young children: Antecedents, correlates, and consequences. *Journal of Personality*, 71:1087–1112.

Kramer, D. (2005). Commentary: Gene-environment interplay in the context of genetics, epigenetics, and gene expression. *Journal of the American Academy of Child and Adolescent Psychiatry*, 44:19–27.

Kruger, D. (2003). Evolution and altruism: Combining psychological mediators with naturally selected tendencies. *Evolution and Human Behavior*, 24:118–125.

Laham, S., K. Gonsalkorale, & W. von Hippel (2005). Darwinian grandparenting: Preferential investment in more certain kin. *Personality and Social Psychology Bulletin*, 31:63–72.

Lanier, M. & S. Henry (2010). *Essential criminology* (3rd ed.). New York: Westview.

Lauritsen, J., K. Heimer, & J. Lynch. (2009). Trends in the gender gap in violent offending: New evidence from the National Crime Victimization Surveys. Criminology, 47:361–399.

Lehmann, L. & L. Keller (2006). The evolution of cooperation and altruism—a general framework and classification of models. *European Society for Evolutionary Biology*, 19:1365–1376.

Leonard, E. (1995). Theoretical criminology and gender. In B. Price & N. Sokoloff (Eds.), *The criminal justice system and women: Offenders, victims, and workers* (pp. 54–70). New York: McGraw-Hill.

Lerner, G. (1986). *The creation of patriarchy.* New York: Oxford University Press.

Levenson, G., C. Patrick, M. Bradley, & P. Lang (2000). The psychopath as observer: Emotion and attention in picture processing. *Journal of Abnormal Psychology*, 109:373–385.

Levy, F., D. Hay, K. Bennett, & M. McStephen (2005). Gender differences in ADHD subtype comorbidity. *Journal of the American Academy of Child and Adolescent Psychiatry*, 44:368–376.

Li, C., X. Mao, & L. Wei (2008). Genes and (common) pathways underlying drug addiction. *PLoS Computational Biology*, 4:28–34.

Lindenfors P. (2005). Neocortex evolution in primates: the 'social brain' is for females. Biology Letters, 1:407–410.

Lindenfors, P., C. Nunn, & R. Barton (2006). Primate brain architecture and selection in relation to sex. *BioMedCentral Biology*, 5:1–9.

Lippa, R. (2002). *Gender, nature, and nurture.* Mahwah, NJ: Lawrence Erlbaum.

Lipset, D. (2003). Rereading Sex and Temperament: Margaret Mead's Sepik triptych and its ethnographic critics. *Anthropological Quarterly*, 76:693–713.

Lober, J. (1994). *The paradoxes of gender.* New Haven, CT: Yale University Press.

Lodi-Smith, J. & B. Roberts (2007). Social investment and personality: A meta-analytic analysis of the relationship of personality traits to investment in work, family, religion, and volunteerism. *Personality and Social Psychology Review*, 11:68–86.

Lopreato, J. & T. Crippen (1999). *Crisis in sociology: The need for Darwin.* New Brunswick, NJ: Transaction.

Lubinski, D. & Humphreys, L. (1997). Incorporating intelligence into epidemiology and the social sciences. *Intelligence*, 24:159–201.

Luders, E., K. Narr, E. Zaidel, P. Thompson, L. Jancke, & A. Toga (2006). Parasagital asymmetries of the corpus callosum. *Cerebral Cortex*, 16:346–354.

Lykken, D. (1995). *The Antisocial Personalities.* Hillsdale, NJ: Lawrence Erlbaum.

MacDonald, K. & T. MacDonald (2010). The peptide that binds: A systematic review of oxytocin and its prosocial effects in humans. *Harvard Review of Psychiatry*, 18:1–21.

Macionis, J. (1989). *Sociology*. Englewood Cliffs, NJ: Prentice Hall.

McBurnett, K., B. Lahey, P. Rathouz, & R. Loeber (2000). Low salivary cortisol and persistent aggression in boys referred for disruptive behavior. *Archives of General Psychiatry*, 57:38–43.

Manica, A. & R. Johnstone (2004). The evolution of paternal care with overlapping broods. *The American Naturalist*, 164:517–530.

Mann, C. (1995). Women of color and the criminal justice system. In B. Price & N. Sokoloff (Eds.), *The criminal justice system and women: Offenders, victims, and workers* (pp. 118–119). New York: McGraw-Hill.

Mann, C. (1988). Getting even? Women who kill in domestic encounters. *Justice Quarterly*, 5, 33–51.

Martin, S. (2001). The links between alcohol, crime and the criminal justice system: Explanations, evidence and interventions. *The American Journal on Addictions*, 10:136–158.

Marx, K. (1978). Economic and philosophical manuscripts of 1844. pp. 66–123, The *Marx-Engels reader*, R. Tucker (Ed.). New York: W.W. Norton.

Massey, D.S. (2002). A brief history of human society: The origin and role of emotions in social life. *American Sociological Review*, 67, 1–29.

Maughan, B., R. Rowe, J. Messer, R. Goodman, & H. Meltzer (2004). Conduct disorder and oppositional defiant disorder in a national sample: Developmental epidemiology. *Journal of Child Psychology and Psychiatry*, 43:609–621.

Mazur, A. & A. Booth (1998). Testosterone and dominance in men. *Behavioral and Brain Sciences*, 21:353–397.

McCrae, T. & A. Terracciano (2005). Universal features of personality traits from the observer's perspective: Data from 50 cultures. *Journal of Personality and Social Psychology*, 88:547–561.

McGue, M. (1999). The behavioral genetics of alcoholism. *Current Directions in Psychological Science*, 8:109–115.

McIntyre, M. & C. Edwards (2009). The early development of gender differences. *Annual Review of Anthropology*, 38:83–97.

Mead, M. (1935). *Sex and Temperament in Three Primitive Societies*. New York: Morrow.

Mead, M. (1949). *Male and Female: A Study of the Sexes in a Changing World*. New York: Morrow.

Mealey, L. (1995). The sociobiology of sociopathy: An integrated evolutionary model. *Behavioral and Brain Sciences*, 18:523–541.

Mealey, L. (2000). *Sex differences: Developmental and evolutionary strategies.* London: Academic Press.

Mealey, L. (2003). Combating Rape: Views of an Evolutionary Psychologist. In R. Bloom and N. Dess, eds., *Evolutionary Psychology and Violence, Westport, Connecticut: Praeger.* pp. 83–113.

Mekel-Bobrov, N., S. Gilbert, P. Evans, E. Vallender, J. Anderson, R. Hudson, S. Tishkoff, & B. Lahn (2005). Ongoing Adaptive Evolution of *ASPM*, a Brain Size Determinant in *Homo Sapiens. Science,* 309:1720–1722.

Mendonca, B., M, Inacio, E. Costa, A. Maria Frade, J. Ivo, D. Russell, & J. Wilson (2003). Male pseudohermaphroditism due to 5[alpha]-reductase 2 deficiency: Outcome of a Brazilian cohort. *The Endocrinologist,* 13:201–204.

Messerschmidt, J. (1993). *Masculinities and Crime: Critique and Reconceptuatlization of Theory*: Lanham, MD: Rowan & Littlefield.

Messerschmidt, J. (2002). On gang girls, gender and a structured action theory. *Theoretical Criminology,* 6:461–475.

Meyer-Bahlburg, H. (2005). Gender identity outcome in female-raised 46,XY persons with penile agenesis, cloacal exstrophy of the bladder, or penile ablation. *Archives of sexual behavior,* 34:423–38.

Meyer-Bahlburg, H., C. Dolezal, S. Baker, A. Ehrhardt, & M. New (2006). Gender development in women with congenital adrenal hyperplasia as a function of disorder severity. *Archives of Sexual Behavior,* 35:667–684.

Michalski, R. & T. Shackelford (2005). Grandparental investment as a function of relational uncertainty and emotional closeness with parents. *Human Nature,* 16:293–305.

Mill, J., A. Caspi, B. Williams, I. Craig, A. Taylor, M. Polo-Tomas, C. Berridge, R. Poulton, & T. Moffitt (2006). Genetic polymorphisms in the dopamine system predict heterogeneity in intelligence and adult prognosis among children with attention-deficit hyperactivity disorder: Evidence from two birth cohorts. *Archives of General Psychiatry,* 63:462–469.

Miller, G. (2007). Sexual selection for moral virtues. *The Quarterly Journal of Biology,* 82:97–125.

Miller, J. (1998). Up it up: Gender and the accomplishment of street robbery. *Criminology,* 36:37–65.

Miller, L. (1987). Neuropsychology of the aggressive psychopath: An integrative review. *Aggressive Behavior,* 13:119–140.

Miller, J. & D. Lynham (2001). Structural models of personality and their relation to antisocial behavior: A meta-analytic review. *Criminology,* 39:765–798.

Miller, W. (1958). Lower-class culture as a generating milieu of gang delinquency. *Journal of Social Issues,* 14:5–19.

Mikkola, M. (2008). Feminist perspectives on sex and gender. *Stanford Ency-clopedia of Philosophy.* Online at http://plato.stanford.edu/entrie/feminism-gender/.

Mitchell, K. (2007). The genetics of brain wiring: From molecule to mind. *PLoS Biology,* 4:690–692.

Moffitt, T., A. Caspi, M. Rutter, & P. Silva (2001). *Sex differences in antisocial behaviour: Conduct disorder, delinquency and violence in the Dunedin longitudinal study.* Cambridge: Cambridge University Press.

Moffitt, T., D. Lynam, & P. Silva (1994). Neuropsychological tests predicting persistent male delinquency. *Criminology,* 32:277–300.

Moll, J., F. Krueger, R. Zahn, M. Pardini, R. de Oliveira-Souza & J. Grafman (2006). Human fronto-mesolimbic networks guide decisions about charitable donation. *Proceedings of the National Academy of Sciences of the United States of America,* 103:15623–15628.

Money, J. (1986). *Venuses Penuses: Sexology, Sexosophy, and Exigency Theory.* Buffalo: NY: Prometheus.

Morris, A. (1987). *Women and Criminal Justice.* Oxford: Basil Blackwell.

Morse, R. & D. Flavin (1992). The definition of alcoholism. The Joint Committee of the National Council on Alcoholism and Drug Dependence and the American Society of Addiction Medicine to Study the Definition and Criteria for the Diagnosis of Alcoholism. *JAMA :The Journal of the American Medical Association* 268:1012–1014.

Nayak, J., B. Sarkar, P. Das, & V. Rao (2008). Genetics of alcohol use in humans: An overview. *International Journal of Human Genetics,* 8:181–197.

Nettler, G. (1982*). Explaining criminals.* Cincinnati, Anderson.

Nettle, D. (2007). Empathizing and systemizing: What are they, and what do they contribute to our understanding of psychological sex differences? *British Journal of Psychology,* 98:237–255.

Neubauer, A. & A. Fink (2009). Intelligence and neural efficiency. *Neuroscience and Biobehavioral Reviews,* 33:1004–1023.

Nicholson, L. (1994). Interpreting gender. *Signs,* 20:79–105.

Norden, J. (2007). *Understanding the brain.* Chantilly, VA: The Teaching Company.

O'Brien, G. (2006). Behavioural phenotypes: Causes and clinical implications. *Advances in Psychiatric Treatment,* 12:338–348.

O'Leary, M., B. Loney, & L. Eckel (2007). Gender differences in the association between psychopathic personality traits and cortisol response to induced stress. *Psychoneuroendocrinology,* 32:183–191.

Oscar-Berman, M., M. Valmas, K. Sawyer, S. Kirkley, D. Gansler, D. Merritt, & A. Couture (2009). Frontal brain dysfunction in alcoholism with and without antisocial personality disorder. *Neuropsychiatric Disease and Treatment*, 5:309–326.

Osgood, D. & J. Chamber (2003). Community correlates of rural youth violence. *Juvenile Justice Bulletin*, May. U.S. Department of Justice.

Owen, T. (2006). Genetic-social science and the study of human biotechnology. *Current Sociology*, 54:897–917.

Parsons, L & D. Osherson (2001). New evidence for distinct right and left brain systems for deductive versus probabilistic reasoning. *Cerebral Cortex*, 11:954–965.

Patrick, C. (1994). Emotions and psychopathy: Startling new insights. *Psychophysiology*, 31:319–330.

Paus, T., I. Nawaz-Khan, G. Leonard, M.Perron, G. Pike, L. Richer, E. Susman, S. Veillette, & Z. Pausova (2010). Sexual dimorphism in the adolescent brain: Role of testosterone and androgen receptor in global and local volumes of grey and white matter. *Hormones and Behavior*, 57:63–75.

Perry, B. (2002). Childhood experience and the expression of genetic potential: What childhood neglect tells us about nature and nurture. *Brain and Mind*, 3:79–100.

Piliavin, J. (2009). Altruism and helping: The evolution of a field: The 2008 Cooley-Mead Presentation. *Social Psychology Quarterly*, 72:209–225.

Piper, G. & S. Schnepf (2008). Gender differences in charitable giving in Great Britian. *Voluntas*, 19:103–124.

Pitchford, I. (2001). The origins of violence: Is psychopathy and adaptation? *Human Nature Review*, 1:28–38.

Platek, S. & T. Shackelford, Eds. (2006). *Female infidelity and paternal uncertainty: Evolutionary perspectives on male anti-cuckoldry tactics.* Cambridge: Cambridge University Press

Plavcan, J. & C. van Schaik (1997). Intrasexual competition and body weight dimorphism in anthropoid primates. *American Journal of Physical Anthropology*, 103:37–68.

Plomin, R., K. Ashbury, & J. Dunn (2001). Why are children in the same family so different? Nonshared environment a decade later. *Canadian Journal of Psychiatry*, 46:225–233.

Plomin, R., (2003). General cognitive ability. In Plomin, R., J. Defries, I. Craig, & P. McGuffin (Eds.), *Behavioral genetics in the postgenomic Era*, pp. 183–201. Washington, DC: American Psychological Association.

Pratt, T. & F. Cullen (2000). The empirical status of Gottfredson and Hirschi's general theory of crime: A meta-analysis. *Criminology*, 38:931–964.

Prescott, C. (2002). Sex differences in the genetic risk for alcoholism. *Alcohol Research & Health*, 26:264–274.

Quartz, S. & T. Sejnowski (1997). The neural basis of cognitive development: A constructivist manifesto. *Behavioral and Brain Sciences*, 20:537–596.

Quinlan, R. & M. Quinlan (2007). Evolutionary ecology of human pair bonds: Cross cultural tests of alternative hypotheses. *Cross-Cultural Research*, 41:149–169.

Qvarnstrom, A., J. Brommer, & L. Gustafsson (2006). Testing the genetics underlying the co-evolution of mate choice and ornament in the wild. *Nature*, 44:84–86.

Raine, A. (1997). Antisocial behavior and psychophysiology: A biosocial perspective and a prefrontal dysfunction hypothesis. In Stoff, D., J. Breiling, & J. Maser (Eds.), *Handbook Of Antisocial Behavior*, pp. 289–304. New York: John Wiley.

Raine, A. & Y. Yang (2006). The neuroanatomical bases of psychopathy: A review of brain imaging findings. In C. Patrick (Ed.), *Handbook of psychopathy*, pp. 278–295. New York: The Guilford Press.

Rasche, C. (1995). Minority women and domestic violence: The unique dilemmas of battered women of color. In B. Price & N. Sokoloff (Eds.), *The criminal justice system and women: Offenders, victims, and workers* (pp. 246–261). New York: McGraw-Hill.

Rennison, C. (2009). New look at the gender gap in offending. *Women and Criminal Justice*, 19-171–190.

Reckdenwald, A. & K. Parker (2008). The influence of gender inequality and marginalization on types of female offending. *Homicide Studies*, 12-208–226.

Reulbach U., T. Biermann, S. Bleich, T. Hillemacher, J. Kornhuber, & W. Sperling (2007). Alcoholism and homicide with respect to the classification systems of Lesch and Cloninger. *Alcohol and Alcoholism*, 42:103–107.

Rhee, S. & I. Waldman (2002). Genetic and environmental influences on antisocial behavior A meta-analysis of twin and adoption studies. *Psychological Bulletin*, 128:490–529.

Richter-Levin, G. (2004). The amygdala, the hippocampus, and emotional modulation of memory. *The Neuroscientist*, 10:31–39.

Ridley, M. (2003). *Nature via nurture: Genes, experience and what makes us human*. New York: Harper Collins.

Ritchie, B. (1996). *Compelled to crime: The gender entrapment of battered black women*. New York: Routledge.

Robinson, M. (2004). *Why crime? An integrated systems theory of antisocial behavior*. Upper Saddle River, NJ: Prentice Hall.

Rogstad, J. & R. Rogers (2008). Gender differences in contributions of emotions to psychopathy and antisocial personality disorder. *Clinical Psychology Review*, 28:1472–1484.

Romaine, C. & C. Reynolds (2005). A model of the development of frontal lobe functioning: Findings from a meta-analysis. *Applied Neuropsychology*, 12:190–201.

Roscoe, P. (2003). Margaret Mead, Reo Fortune, and Mountain Apapesh warfare. *American Anthropologist*, 105:581–591.

Rosario, V. (2009). Quantum sex: Intersex and the molecular deconstruction of sex. *GLO: A Journal of Lesbian and Gay Studies*, 15:267–284.

Rose, S. (1999). Precis of *Lifelines:* Biology, freedom, determinism. *Behavioral and Brain Sciences*, 22:871–921.

Rose, S. (2001). Moving on from old dichotomies: Beyond nature-nurture towards a lifeline perspective. *British Journal of Psychiatry*, 178:3–7.

Rosenfeld, R. (2000). Patterns in adult homicide. In Blumstein, A. & J. Wallman (Eds.), *The Crime Drop in America*, pp. 130–163. Cambridge: Cambridge University Press.

Rossi, A. (1984). Gender and Parenthood. *American Sociological Review*, 49:1–19.

Rowe, D. (1996). An adaptive strategy theory of crime and delinquency. In J. Hawkins (Ed.), *Delinquency and crime: Current theories*, pp. 268–314. Cambridge: Cambridge University Press.

Rowe, D. (2002). *Biology and crime*. Los Angeles: Roxbury.

Ruden, R. (1997). *The craving brain: The biobalance approach to controlling addictions*. New York: Harper Collins.

Rushton, J., D. Fulker, M. Neale, D. Nias, & H. Eysenk (1986). Altruism and aggression: The heritability of individual differences. *Journal of Personality and Social Psychology*, 50:1192–1198.

Sanderson, S. (2001). *The evolution of human sociality: A Darwinian conflict perspective*. Lanham, MD: Rowman & Littlefield.

Sasi, R. (2010). Attention-deficit hyperactivity disorder and gender. *Archives of Women's Mental Health*, 13:29–31.

Sayer, A. (1997). Essentialism, social constructionism, and beyond. *Sociological Review*, 45:453–487.

Sayers, S. (2005). Why work? Marx and human nature. *Science & Society*, 69:606–616.

Sax, L. (2006). Six degrees of separation: What teachers need to know about the emerging science of sex differences. *Educational Horizons*, 84:190–212.

Scarpa, A. & A. Raine (2003). The psychophysiology of antisocial behavior: Interactions with environmental experiences. In Walsh, A. & L. Ellis (Eds.). *Biosocial criminology: Challenging environmentalism's supremacy*, pp. 209–226. Hauppauge, NY: Nova Science.

Schulte-Ruther, M., H. Markowitsch, G. Fink, & M. Piefke (2007). Mirror neuron and theory of mind mechanisms involved in face-to-face interactions: A functional magnetic resonance imaging approach to empathy. *Journal of Cognitive Neuroscience*, 19:1354–1472.

Schmitt, D., A. Realo, M. Voracek, & J. Allik (2008). Why can't a man be more like a woman? Sex differences in big five personality traits across 55 cultures. *Journal of Personality and Social Psychology*, 94:168–182.

Schwartz, J., D. Steffensmeier, H. Zhong, & J. Ackerman. (2009). Trends in the gender gap in violence: Reevaluating NCVS and other evidence. *Criminology* 47:401–426.

Schmallager, F. (2006). *Criminology Today*. Upper Saddle River, NJ: Prentice Hall.

Schon, R. & M. Silven (2007). Natural parenting—back to basics in infant care. *Evolutionary Psychology*, 5:102–183.

Schulte-Rüther, M., H. Markowitsch, N. Shah, G. Fink, & M. Piefke (2008). Gender differences in brain networks supporting empathy. *NeuroImage*, 42:393–403.

Serran, G. & P. Firestone (2004). Intimate partner homicide: A review of the male proprietariness and self-defense theories. *Aggression and Violent Behavior*, 9:1–15.

Shah, B. (2009). A challenge to "malestream" determinism. http://www.docs toc.com/docs/12115436/WOMENS-WRITING.

Shea, C. (2009). The nature-nurture debate, redux: Genetic research finally makes its way into the thinking of sociologists. *Chronicle of Higher Education: Chronicle Review*. http://chronicle.com/free/v55/i18/18b00601.htm. January, 9:B6.

Shelden, R., S. Tracy, & W. Brown (2001). *Youth gangs in American society* (2nd Ed.). Belmont, CA: Wadsworth.

Siegel, L. (1992). *Criminology, 4th edition*, St. Paul, MN: West Publishing.

Silfver, M., K. Helkama, J. Lonnqvist, & M. Verkasalo (2008). The relation between value priorities and proneness to guilt, shame, and empathy. *Motivation and Emotion*, 32:69–80.

Silfver, M. & H. Klaus (2007). Empathy, guilt, and gender: A comparison of two measures of guilt. *Scandinavian Journal of Psychology*, 48:239–246.

Silverman, I., J. Choi, & M. Peters (2007). The hunter-gatherer theory of sex differences in spatial abilities: Data from 40 countries. Archives of Sexual Behavior, 36:261–268.

Simon, R. (1975). *Women and Crime*. Lexington, MA: Lexington Books.

Sisk, C. & J. Zehr (2005). Pubertal hormones organize the adolescent brain and behavior. *Frontiers in Neuroendocrinology*, 26:163–174.

Slaght, E., S. Lyman, & S. Lyman (2004). Promoting healthy lifestyles as a biopsychosocial approach to addictions counseling. *Journal of Alcohol & Drug Education*, 48, 5–16.

Smart, C. (1976). *Women, crime and criminology: A feminist critique.* London: Routledge & Kegan Paul.

Sokoloff, N. & B. Price (1995). The criminal law and women. In Price, B. & N. Sokoloff (Eds.), *The Criminal justice system and women: Offenders, victims, and workers,* pp. 11–29. New York: McGraw-Hill.

Sowell, T. (1987). *A conflict of visions: Ideological origins of political struggles.* New York: William Morrow.

Spelman, W. (2000). The limited importance of prison expansion. In Blumstein, A. & J. Wallman (Eds.), *The Crime Drop in America,* pp. 97–129. Cambridge: Cambridge University Press.

Spergel, I. (1995). *The youth gang problem: A community approach.* New York: Oxford University Press.

Spiro, M. (1975). *Children of the Kibbutz.* Cambridge: Harvard University Press.

Spiro, M. (1980). *Gender and Culture: Kibbutz Women Revisited.* New York: Schocken.

Spiro, M. (1999). Anthropology and human nature. *Ethos,* 27:7–14.

Steffensmeier, D. & E. Allan (1996). Gender and crime: Toward a gendered theory of female offending. *Annual Review of Sociology,* 22:459:488.

Steffensmeier, D. & D. Haynie (2000). Gender, structural disadvantage, and urban crime: Do macrosocial variables also explain female offending rates? *Criminology* 38:403–438.

Steffensmeier, D. H. Zhong, J. Ackerman, J. Schwartz, & S. Agha (2006). Gender gap trends for violent crimes, 1980 to 2003: A UCR-NCVS comparison. *Feminist Criminology,* 1:71–98.

Steimer, T. (2002). The biology of fear- and anxiety-related behaviors. *Dialogues in Clinical Neurosciences,* 4:231–249.

Stone, B. (2001). Liberalism and the science of human nature. *Society,* 38:71–78.

Storey, A., K. Delahunty, D. McKay, C. Walsh, & S. Wilhelm (2006). Social and hormonal bases for individual differences in the parental behaviour of birds and mammals. *Canadian Journal of Experimental Psychology,* 60, 237–245.

Substance Abuse and Mental Health Services Administration, Office of Applied Studies. (2007). *The NSDUH Report: Gender Differences in Alcohol Use and Alcohol Dependence or Abuse: 2004 and 2005.* Rockville, MD.

Swaab, D. (2004). Sexual differentiation of the human brain: Relevance for gender identity, transsexualism and sexual orientation. *Gynecological Endocrinology,* 19:301–312.

Taylor, S. (2006). Tend and Befriend: Biobehavioral bases of affiliation under stress. *Current Directions in Psychological Science.* 15:273–277.

Taylor, S., L. Klien, B. Lewis, T. Gruenwald, R. Gurung, & J. Updegraff (2000). Biobehavioral responses to stress in females: Tend-and-befriend, not fight-or-flight. *Psychological Review.* 107:411–429.

Terranova, A., A. Morris, & P. Boxer (2008). Fear reactivity and effortful control in overt and relational bullying: A six-month longitudinal study. *Aggressive Behavior*, 34:104–115.

Thorne, B. (1993). Gender play: Girls and boys in school. New Brunswick, NJ: Rutgers University Press.

Tinbergen, N. (1963). On aims and methods in ethology. *Zeitschrift für Tierpsychologie*, 20:410–433.

Trautner, H. (1992). The development of sex-typing in children. *German Journal of Psychology*, 16:183–199.

Trivers, R. (1971). The evolution of reciprocal altruism. *Quarterly Review of Biology*, 46:35–57.

Trudge, C. (1999). Who's afraid of genetic determinism? *Biologist*, 46:96.

Unger, R. (1996). Using the master's tools: Epistemology and *empiricism*. In S. Wilkinson (Ed.), *Feminist social psychologies: International perspectives*, pp. 165–181. Milton Keynes, England: Open University Press.

Udry, R. (1994). The nature of gender. *Demography*, 31:561–573.

van As, A., G. Fieggen, & P. Tobias (2007). Sever abuse of infants—an evolutionary price for human development? *South African Journal of Children's Health*, 1:54–57.

van Bokhoven, I., S. van Goozen, H. Engeland, B. Schaal, L. Arseneault, J. Seguin, J. Assaad, D. Nagin, F. Vitaro, & R. Tremblay (2006). Salivary testosterone and aggression, delinquency, and social dominance, in a population-based longitudinal study of adolescent males. *Hormones and Behavior*, 50:118–125.

van den Berghe, P. (1990). Why most sociologists don't (and won't) think evolutionarily. *Sociological Forum*, 5:173–185.

van Goozen, S., G. Fairchild, H. Snoek, & G. Harold (2007). The evidence for a neurobiological model of childhood antisocial behavior. *Psychological Bulletin*, 133:149–82.

Vandermassen, G. (2004). Sexual selection: A tale of male bias and feminist denial. *The European Journal of Women's Studies*, 11:9–26.

van Voorhees, E. & A. Scarpa (2004). The effects of child maltreatment on the hypothalamic-pituitary-adrenal axis. *Trauma, Violence, and Abuse*, 5:333–352.

Vaughn, M., M. Delisi, K. Beaver, & J. Wright (2009). DAT1 and 5HTT are associated with pathological criminal behavior in a nationally representative sample. *Criminal Justice and Behavior*, 36:1113–1124.

Verona, E. & J. Vitale (2006). Psychopathy in women: Assessment, manifestations, and etiology. In C. Patrick (Ed.), *Handbook of psychopathy*, pp. 415–436. New York: The Guilford Press.

Viding, W., J. Blair, T. Moffitt, & R. Plomin (2005). Evidence for substantial genetic risk for psychopathy in 7-year-olds. *Journal of Child Psychology and Psychiatry*, 46:592–597.

Walderhaug E, A. Magnusson, A. Neumeister, J. Lappalainen, H. Lunde, H. Refsum, & N. Landrø (2007). Interactive effects of sex and 5-HTTLPR on mood and impulsivity during tryptophan depletion in healthy people. *Biological Psychiatry*, 62:593–599.

Wallis D, H. Russell, & M. Muenke (2008). Review: Genetics of attention deficit/hyperactivity disorder. *Journal of Pediatric Psychology*, 33:8:6–12.

Waldman, L. & S. Rhee (2006). Gene and environmental influences on psychopathy and antisocial behavior. In C. Patrick (Ed.), *Handbook of psychopathy*, pp. 205–228. New York: The Guilford Press.

Walsh, A. (1995). Genetic and cytogenetic intersex anomalies: Can they help us to understand gender differences in deviant behavior? *International Journal of Offender Therapy and Comparative Criminology*, 39:151–164.

Walsh, A. (2000). Human reproductive strategies and life history theory. In Bancroft, J. (Ed.), *The role of theory in sex research*, pp. 17–29. Bloomington, IN: Indiana University Press.

Walsh, A. (2003). Intelligence and antisocial behavior. In Walsh, A. & L. Ellis (Eds.) *Biosocial criminology: Challenging environmentalism's supremacy.* pp. 105–124. Huntington, NY: Nova Science.

Walsh, A. (2006). Evolutionary psychology and criminal behavior. In J. Barkow (Ed.). *Missing the Revolution: Darwinism for Social Scientists.* pp. 225–268. Oxford: Oxford University Press.

Walsh, A. (2009). *Biology and criminology: The biosocial synthesis.* New York: Routledge.

Walsh, A. & K. Beaver (2008). The Promise of evolutionary psychology for criminology: The examples of gender and age. In J. Duntley & T. Shackleford (Eds.), *Evolutionary Forensic Psychology*. Oxford: Oxford University Press.

Walsh, A. & L. Ellis (2007). *Criminology: An interdisciplinary approach.* Thousand Oaks, CA: Sage.

Walsh, A. & H-H. Wu (2008). Differentiating antisocial personality disorder, psychopathy, and sociopathy: Evolutionary, genetic, neurological, and sociological considerations. *Criminal Justice Studies*, 21:135–152.

Warneken, F. & M. Tomasello (2009). The roots of human altruism. *British Journal of Psychology*, 100:455–471.

Warren, J., S. South, M., Burnette, A. Rogers, R. Friend, R. Bale, & I. Van Patten (2005). Understanding the risk factors for violence and criminality in women: The concurrent validity of the PCL-R and the HCR-20. *International Journal of Law and Psychiatry, 28,* 269–289.

Waschbusch, D., W. Pelham Jr., J. Jennings, A. Greiner, R. Tarter, & H. Moss (2002). Reactive aggression in boys with disruptive behavior disorders: behavior, physiology, and affect *Journal of Abnormal Child Psychology,* 30:641–656.

Watters, E. (2006). DNA is not destiny. *Discover: Science, Technology and the Future.* November.

Wechsler, D. (1958). *The measurement and appraisal of adult intelligence.* Baltimore: Williams and Wilkin.

Weinhold, B. (2006). Epigenetics: The science of change. *Environmental Health Perspectives,* 114:161–167.

Wells, B. (1980). *Personality and heredity.* London: Longman.

Wexler, B. (2006). *Brain and culture: Neurobiology, ideology, and social change.* Cambridge, MA: MIT Press.

Wiebe, R. (2004). Psychopathy and sexual coercion: A Darwinian analysis. *Counseling and Clinical Psychology Journal,* 1:23–41.

Wiebe, R. (2009). Psychopathy. In Walsh, A. & K. Beaver (Eds.), *Biosocial criminology: New directions in theory and research,* pp. 224–242. New York: Routledge.

Williams, L., M. Barton, A. Kemp., B. Liddell, A. Peduto, E. Gordon, & R. Bryant (2005). Distinct amygdala-autonomic arousal profiles in response to fear signals in healthy males and females. *NeuroImage,* 28:618–626.

Wilson, E.O. (1998). *Consilience: The unity of knowledge.* New York: Alfred A.

Wilson, J. & R. Herrnstein (1985). *Crime and human nature.* New York: Simon & Schuster.

Witt, L., L. Burke, M. Barrick, & M. Mount (2002). The interactive effects of conscientiousness and agreeableness on job performance. *Journal of Applied Psychology,* 87:164–169.

Wood, W. & A. Eagly (2002). A cross-cultural analysis of the behavior of women and men: Implications for the origins of sex difference. *Psychological Bulletin, 128,* 699–727.

Woo, L., J. Thomas, & J. Brock (2009). Cloacal exstrophy: A comprehensive review of an uncommon problem. *Journal of Pediatric Urology.*

Wright, J. & P. Boisvert (2009). What biosocial criminology offers criminology. *Criminal Justice and Behavior,* 36:1228–1239.

Wrong, D. (1961). The oversocialized conception of man in modern sociology. American Sociological Review, 26:183–193.

Xu, J. & C. Disteche (2006). Sex differences in brain expression of X- and Y-linked genes. *Brain Research*, 1126:50–55.

Yamasue, H., O. Abe, M. Suga, H. Yamada, M. Rogers, A. Shigeki, N. Kato, & K. Kasai (2008). Sex-linked neuroanatomical basis of human altruistic cooperativeness. Cerebral Cortex, 18:2331–2340.

Yang, J., L. Baskin, & M. DiSandro (2010). Gender identity in disorders of sex development: Review article. *Urology*, 75:153–159.

Zucker, K. (2002). Intersexuality and gender identity differentiation. *Journal of Pediatric Adolescent Gynecology*, 15:3–13.

Zuckerman, M. (2007). *Sensation seeking and risky behavior*. Washington, DC: American Psychological Association.

Index

blank slate: and socialization, 24–25; view of human nature, 46, 56

Bohan, J., 48–49

brain 4, 69–72, 74, 77: and evolutionary changes, 9, 66; and homosexuality, 61; and psychopathy, 80, 120–121; basic development of, 93–95; cells, 108; laterality, 95, 98; masculinization, 86–87, 90; sexual differentiation of, 55, 83–92, 98–99, 109–110, 113–114, 116–117; social, 106; stress impact on male and female, 100–102, 104

C

cad strategy, 80

cad vs. dad, 81

Carlen, P., 28

causation: crime, 11, 13; question, 4–5

cerebrum, 95

cheater theory, 78–80

Chesney-Lind, M., 13, 19–20, 22

chromosome, 68, 85–87

cloacal exstrophy, 90–91

Cloward, R., 15–16

Coleman, J., 50

Coleridge, S., 92

conditional adaptation theory (CAT), 78, 81

conduct disorder: and gender differences, 21, 116, 118

congenital adrenal hyperplasia (CAH), 88

conscientiousness, 111–112

convergence hypothesis, 29–30, 39

corpus callosum, 95

cortisol, 88, 101; hypercortisolism, 101–102; hypocortisolism, 102

crime rates: and power control theory, 34; by gender, 16–17, 21–22, 24, 28–30, 40

Cronin, H., 42, 54

cuckoldry, 8

Cullen, F., 3

D

dad strategy, 80

Darwin, C., 67: framework, 5, 63, 65, 72, 106; feminists, 8–9, 67

DAX-1, 85

de Waal, F., 107

delinquent peers, 37

denys-drash syndrome (DDS), 86

determinism, 43, 45–46; biological, 49; cultural, 56; strong cultural, 60, 64

development, 21; and ADHD/CD, 114–115; of basic brain, 93–94; of children, 5–27, 70; of gender differences, 39, 41, 71, 85, 88, 96, 106; of personality, 60; of psychopathy, 120; question, 4–5, 24

diethylstilbestrol (DES), 88

differential association, 13, 16–17

dopamine, 115, 117

dopamine receptor (DRD4), 115

dopamine transporter (DAT1), 79, 115

E

economic marginalization hypothesis, 29

effortful control, 113–114

egalitarian family, 34–35

egotism, 105

Ehrenreich, B., 55